W9-BNP-578

More Praise for *Trust and Betrayal in the Workplace*

"Better than anyone else, the Reinas are bringing the human side of the equation back into our organizations. They're showing us that trust isn't a feeling but a tangible element that influences how we interact. The Reinas have ventured into territory where no one has gone before in this third edition."

—**Eric Deschenes, Vice President, Canada Segments and Targeted Customers, and Vice President, Energy Business for Canada, Schneider Electric Canada Inc.**

"This third edition breaks through theory into our personal realities to reveal the possibility each one of us has to build or rebuild trust in our workplaces and lives. It is personal, universal, relevant to all aspects of life, and deeply empowering: a timely, accessible gift."

—**Katherine Armstrong, Director, Business Transformation, Volac International, United Kingdom**

"A powerful, insightful, yet accessible approach to understanding the impact when trust is broken—both at home and in the workplace. The Seven Steps for Healing provide a framework that empowers you to take responsibility, identify when and why trust was broken, and restore trust again. This third edition is filled with useful lessons."

—**Heidi Dross, Senior Director, Group Benefits, Aetna Health Insurance**

"In this third edition of *Trust and Betrayal in the Workplace*, both leaders and followers are given a fresh perspective on trust. This is not an update; rather, it's a new book written not only for management but also for every person in the whole organization."

—**Thomas C. Johnston, Dean, New England School of Communications, Husson University**

"In this latest edition, the Reinas have demonstrated that trust is the foundation for all relationships, both in the workplace and in our everyday lives. They've taught us how to make trustworthy connections so we can create an environment where teamwork flourishes and people want to work."

—**Landon Cobb, CPA, FLMI, Chief Accounting Officer, Fidelity & Guaranty Life**

"This third edition is a simple approach to a very complex problem. It's about leveraging your strengths to create alignment between who you are, what you love to do, and the relationships you value. This book is the answer to a great need."

—**Susan Harpster, Executive Director, Group Insurance—New Business and Administrative Risk Services, Aetna**

"This third edition of *Trust and Betrayal in the Workplace* offers readers the opportunity to learn the value of trust, the danger of betrayal, and the path to healing and improvement. These concepts are essential to success."

—**Kevin W. Donovan, CEO, Mt. Ascutney Hospital and Health Center**

"In the third edition of *Trust and Betrayal in the Workplace*, Dennis and Michelle Reina present effective insight into the crucial role that trust plays in making an organization successful and sustainable. Trust creates an ethos of sanguinity and alliance that leads to a performance-driven environment. A compelling read!"

—Dr. Saagarika Ghoshal, Director, Human Resources, Metro Cash and Carry, Bengaluru, India

"Powerfully and beautifully written, this new edition of *Trust and Betrayal in the Workplace* is full of valuable instruction, meaningful stories, and practical guidance, as well as being a real pleasure to read. After reading it, I am convinced that strengthening trust will allow us to unlock greater success in our workplaces."

—Catherine Robinson-Walker, author of *Leading Valiantly in Healthcare*

"The third edition carries a powerful message: if you want more trust in your relationships with others, first change your own behaviors and actions. More than ever before, sustainable relationships based in trust are a crucial competitive advantage. *Trust and Betrayal in the Workplace* provides actionable techniques to help *you* build and sustain trust."

—Tim Mai, Senior Vice President, LPL Financial

"This book helped me become aware of the subtle erosions of trust in my relationships and equipped me to respond with thoughtfulness and compassion. I'm certain the skills I've learned will give me an advantage when I enter the workplace after graduation."

—Julia Rauen, Sophomore, Echols Scholar, University of Virginia

"In this third edition of *Trust and Betrayal in the Workplace*, you will find an insightful and understandable road map to help you, your colleagues, and your customers build trust and function at your highest levels. Well written and thoroughly relatable, this book is a must-read for any organization and its leaders."

—Kevin McCarthy, President and CEO, PC Construction Company

"Trust is the key issue for our times, and Dennis and Michelle Reina are the go-to experts on trust. Read their brilliant book before trust becomes an issue. You can trust their advice—I do!"

—Jesse Lyn Stoner, coauthor of *Full Steam Ahead!* and *Leading at a Higher Level*

"In this new edition of *Trust and Betrayal in the Workplace*, the Reinas remind us that leaders can't be the sole guides in creating trust: we all have a responsibility to practice healthy, trustworthy behaviors. The Reinas are on to something huge."

—Jay Fayette, Senior Vice President, PC Construction Company

"This new edition of *Trust and Betrayal in the Workplace* is resourceful, timely, and practical. I continue to use the proven and thoughtful strategies in my work. This amazing book is a must-read!"

—Jill C. Dagilis, Executive Director, Worcester Community Action Council, Inc.

‹Third Edition, Revised and Updated ›

Trust and Betrayal in the Workplace

Building Effective Relationships in Your Organization

Dennis Reina, PhD, and Michelle Reina, PhD

BK

Berrett–Koehler Publishers, Inc.
a BK Business book

Copyright © 2015 by Dennis Reina, PhD, and Michelle Reina, PhD

All rights reserved. No part of this publication may be reproduced, distributed, or transmitted in any form or by any means, including photocopying, recording, or other electronic or mechanical methods, without the prior written permission of the publisher, except in the case of brief quotations embodied in critical reviews and certain other noncommercial uses permitted by copyright law. For permission requests, write to the publisher, addressed "Attention: Permissions Coordinator," at the address below.

Berrett-Koehler Publishers, Inc.
1333 Broadway, Suite 1000
Oakland, CA 94612-1921
Tel: (510) 817-2277   Fax: (510) 817-2278   www.bkconnection.com

Ordering Information

Quantity sales. Special discounts are available on quantity purchases by corporations, associations, and others. For details, contact the "Special Sales Department" at the Berrett-Koehler address above.

Individual sales. Berrett-Koehler publications are available through most bookstores. They can also be ordered directly from Berrett-Koehler: Tel: (800) 929-2929; Fax: (802) 864-7626; www.bkconnection.com

Orders for college textbook/course adoption use. Please contact Berrett-Koehler: Tel: (800) 929-2929; Fax: (802) 864-7626.

Orders by U.S. trade bookstores and wholesalers. Please contact Ingram Publisher Services, Tel: (800) 509-4887; Fax: (800) 838-1149; E-mail: customer.service@ingrampublisherservices .com; or visit www.ingrampublisherservices.com/Ordering for details about electronic ordering.

Berrett-Koehler and the BK logo are registered trademarks of Berrett-Koehler Publishers, Inc.

Printed in the United States of America

Berrett-Koehler books are printed on long-lasting acid-free paper. When it is available, we choose paper that has been manufactured by environmentally responsible processes. These may include using trees grown in sustainable forests, incorporating recycled paper, minimizing chlorine in bleaching, or recycling the energy produced at the paper mill.

Library of Congress Cataloging-in-Publication Data
Reina, Dennis S., 1950–
    Trust and betrayal in the workplace : building effective relationships in your organization /
    Dennis Reina, Michelle Reina. -- Third edition, revised and updated.
        pages cm
    Revised edition of Trust & betrayal in the workplace, published in 2006.
    ISBN 978-1-62656-257-8 (pbk.)
    1. Organizational behavior. 2. Trust. 3. Interpersonal relations. 4. Organizational effectiveness. 5. Work environment. 6. Psychology, Industrial. I. Reina, Michelle L., 1958- II. Title. III. Title: Trust & betrayal in the workplace.
    HD58.7.R4388 2015
    158.7--dc23
                                                                                2014039110

Third Edition
20 19 18 17 16 15   10 9 8 7 6 5 4 3 2 1

Interior design and project management: Dovetail Publishing Services
Illustration: Bob von Elgg, Big Fish/Small Pond Design
Cover design: Dan Tesser, Studio Carnelian

To Dennis's mother, Loretta,
And Michelle's mother, Lorraine,
For loving us
And supporting us to explore life,
Take risks,
And learn how to trust in ourselves.

The following expressions are registered trademarks of Reina, A Trust Building Consultancy:

The Reina Trust & Betrayal Model®

Trust Building®

The Three Cs of Trust®

Trust of Character®

Trust of Communication®

Trust of Capability®

Capacity for Trust®

Transformative Trust®

Transforming Workplaces Through Trust®

Trust WorkOuts®

Seven Steps for Healing®

Three Dimensions of Trust: The Three Cs®

Trust Begins with You®

Trust Begins with Me®

For ease of reading, the ® symbols have been removed from the text of this book.

Contents

Preface

This book is about trust: the power when it exists, the pain when it's betrayed, and the transformation that occurs when it's been renewed. Our purpose in completely rewriting the third edition of this book is to help people at *all* levels—not just leaders—of *any* organization create, support, and, if necessary, rebuild trust within themselves and with others.

This book is about creating more productive, engaging, and rewarding work environments for everyone. It's about relationships that are built on trust and infused with spirit—relationships that inspire leaders and employees alike. The principles, tools, and techniques offered in *Trust and Betrayal in the Workplace* apply to anyone, in any kind of relationship, at any level of responsibility, and in any kind of setting—both at work and at home.

More than ever, there is a need for trust in workplace relationships. Organizations and people face increasing challenges; some associated with growth and expansion, others with downsizing or restructuring. Although change and transition have become commonplace, our need for trust-based relationships endures. Why? Because of one simple truth: business is conducted through relationships and trust is the foundation of effective relationships.

Trust builds the bridge between the business need for results and the human need for connection.

Trust is foundational to how you bring yourself to your work and your relationships. Yet, trust is fragile. It takes time to develop, is easy to lose, and is hard to regain. Countless numbers of people in the workplace today suffer from the loss of trust. In fact, after decades of constant change—years of downsizing, restructuring, and reengineering, or of mergers and growth—trust among people at every organizational level is needed more than ever.

You're not immune to this reality. You've personally felt the pain of breached trust from minor letdowns and disappointments. You may even have suffered a major betrayal by another's self-serving action. Unmet expectations, letdowns, broken trust, and even betrayals crop up every day on the job. The hard truth is, these situations impact your performance and the performance of your colleagues.

You can counteract this downward spiral of broken trust and diminished effectiveness by learning to trust more in yourself and others. You can develop caring, genuine relationships based on mutually trustworthy intentions. You can benefit from inspired collaboration, improved performance, and a renewed ability to find joy in your relationships—both at work and at home. You can do these things. Trust begins with you.

Who Should Read This Book

This book is designed to help anyone who has the desire to cultivate trusting relationships with the people with whom they work and live. You may feel that your workplace has a fairly healthy level of trust and you want to build upon it because you know it will give you and your colleagues a competitive edge in the marketplace. Or you may see signs that trust is vulnerable in your organization. The "grapevine" may be in overdrive, relationships may be breaking down, people may not be following through on their commitments, climate survey results may be less than desirable, and people may be leaving the company. Your instincts may be telling you that "something is just not quite right" in your work environment.

Our focus is for anyone at any level of responsibility who values relationships and wants to understand what trust means—how it's built, how it's broken, and how it may be rebuilt in order to create more effective connections. We find that people want trust; they just aren't sure how to go about fostering it. For many, building trust—and more importantly rebuilding it—may seem like an overwhelming task. Here, we help you, and we help you learn how to help those around you.

We explore the specific behaviors that build trusting relationships, pinpoint the behaviors that contribute to subtle and not-so-subtle breaches of trust, and explain the actions you can take to learn to trust again. *Trust and Betrayal in the Workplace* will help you understand and appreciate the complex dynamics of trust and betrayal. Your understanding of trust will be improved—as will your awareness of the variety of ways betrayal occurs and its consequences. This book serves as a comprehensive reference and practical guide to building trust-based relationships between individuals, within and among teams, and throughout organizations—both in good times and in challenging times. You can use what you learn in this book both at work and at home, to connect with others, and to connect with yourself.

Overview of the Book

Understanding the complexity of trust and betrayal is challenging work, yet necessary. We draw upon what we have learned first-hand from life experience, years of research, and work with thousands of people in hundreds of organizations around the world. The topic of trust is emotionally charged and means different things to different people. The Reina Trust & Betrayal Model provides an understandable framework for you to work through this complexity. We make trust concrete and actionable for you by giving you a common language to discuss trust-related issues and act on them in a thoughtful manner. You'll learn to use this language to create and take action to maintain healthy levels of trust in your organization.

Chapter 1, "Trust Begins with You," provides an overview of the book. This overview establishes that people want trust, need trust, and deserve trust. We address trust's importance by exploring the business and human need for it; the price people and organizations pay when it's low; and the payoff when it's high. We clarify that in order to get trust, people must be willing to give it. Trust begins with the individual effort put forth by each one of us. Trust begins with you.

We devote Chapters 2 through 4 to discussing the Three Dimensions of Trust, commonly referred to as "The Three Cs of Trust"—Trust of Character, Trust of Communication, and Trust of Capability. We discuss the specific behaviors that build each type of trust and bring these actions to life to through examples and vignettes culled from our decades of field research and practical experience. We also give you tools, techniques, and tips to practice the behaviors in your relationships on a daily basis.

Chapter 5, "Your Readiness and Willingness to Trust," helps you explore your readiness and willingness to trust in yourself and others. Because trust begins with you, it's vital you develop this understanding of your own Capacity for Trust. Chapter 6, "How You Trust," takes you on a deeper exploration of how, when, and why you trust through the lens of four powerful questions.

In all relationships, trust will be built and trust will be broken. With trust comes betrayal. Chapter 7, "How Trust Is Broken: Betrayal," discusses the word *betrayal* and shares why it's important that you understand it. We talk about the big things as well as the subtle, unintentional, day-to-day occurrences that cause people to feel their trust has been broken. We explore the impact of these betrayals to individuals, relationships, and performance. Chapter 8, "How Trust Is Rebuilt: The Seven Steps," takes you through proven steps to overcome the disappointment and pain of betrayal and learn to trust again.

Chapter 9, "How Trust Is Transformed: Transformative Trust," examines the four catalysts that help you create Transformative Trust: conviction, courage, compassion, and community. We show you how they work, their value, and how you can amplify trust within your individual relationships, your team, and your organization.

Chapter 10, "Taking Trust to the Next Level," takes you on an inner journey through four pathways to deepen your relationship with yourself. These pathways help you remove the barriers that stand between you and building more trust in your relationships. Trust begins with you. Your relationship with yourself is foundational to how you bring yourself to others, both at work and at home.

Throughout this book we guide you to build trust. We provide you with "how-to" charts and action steps; and each chapter concludes with questions enabling you to reflect on your experience and a Trust Tip. You'll walk away with key points to remember and a game plan to put into action on your trust building journey.

Development of This Book

This book first took root many years ago when we were working with organizations to design and develop teams, manage change, strengthen leadership credibility, and build managerial strategies. Leaders would ask us to help them understand why their development efforts were not producing results. When we reached out to their people for insight, again and again we would hear that lack of results were due to the breakdown of trust—a breakdown of trust among co-workers, with bosses, in teams, and throughout the organization.

We went on a search for solutions. Being doctoral students at the time, we each committed to studying elements of trust in our respective dissertations. We learned a great deal about trust and how central it is in relationships and organizations. We were, however, left with more questions than answers. Our quest continued.

The next phase of our research brought us to sixty-seven organizations in nineteen industries. We learned that it was not possible for people to talk about trust without talking about betrayal and the need to recover from it. The outgrowth of those early years of work experience and research gave birth to the Reina Trust & Betrayal Model, which served as the framework for the first edition of our first book. The purpose of the first edition of *Trust and Betrayal in the Workplace* was to provide a working construct of trust, betrayal, and rebuilding trust. The second edition was an expansion with a focus on helping leaders, in particular, learn to trust themselves and others more as they led organizations in a dynamic, complicated marketplace. Since the publication of the second edition, the cries for a trusting workplace have become louder and louder. We have listened and have dug even deeper to understand all aspects of trust.

Hands-on experience in hundreds of organizations and with thousands of leaders, managers, supervisors, human resource professionals, and front-line employees in a multitude of functions have taught us that although leaders do have significant responsibility to cultivate a culture of high trust, they do not have 100 percent responsibility. Each and every individual has responsibility for his or her part in building trust within their relationships throughout their organization. Trust begins with you. Trust begins with each and every one of us.

This third edition of *Trust and Betrayal in the Workplace* has been rewritten and refocused for you—regardless of your rank or responsibility level in your organization. Our intent is to help you build sustainable trust in your relationships, in your teams, and throughout the organization you serve. The stories and quotes in the book come from the actual experiences lived by people and shared with us in our research and work. The names and locations of individuals and organizations have been changed to maintain anonymity and to protect their trust in us.

We all have experiences of trust and betrayal. In our service to organizations, we continue to learn about trust. What we've learned from our clients and our lives is shared with you in the pages of this book. We also share personal stories of our own. Our interest in trust is passionate. Our professional lives are devoted to supporting the cultivation of trust in relationships all over the world. We believe that all human beings deserve to trust in themselves and to feel safe to trust in others. We wrote this book and continue our work to that end.

Dennis Reina, PhD
Michelle Reina, PhD
Stowe, Vermont
July 2014

CHAPTER ONE

Trust Begins with You

Alex was head of a beverage manufacturing plant that was the lowest producer of thirteen plants nationwide.

By focusing entirely on bottom-line results, Alex had missed the biggest obstacle standing in the way of his organization reaching peak performance: a failure to build trusting relationships with his people. Although Alex cared a great deal about his employees, they didn't know it. He focused on the numbers and neglected to ask them what they needed to be successful in their jobs. They didn't think he cared about them, their issues, or their concerns. As a result, trust, morale, and production were at an all-time low.

Once Alex learned how to earn the trust of his employees and helped his employees learn how to build trusting relationships with one another, productivity soared. Within two years, the plant went from being the lowest to highest producer out of all thirteen plants. Alex and his team went on to win his organization's most coveted award, the Manufacturing Excellence of the Year Award.

We're all challenged in our efforts to connect with our colleagues, bosses, and employees—especially when we feel that we can't trust them or they don't trust us. You hold this book in your hands because your gut is telling you that in order to bring your work, relationships, and organization to the next level, you need to learn how to give trust, get it, and be equipped to repair it when it's been broken. You want trust. You need trust. You deserve trust.

The good news is, trust begins with you: with your attitudes, your intentions, and your behaviors within your relationships. This is good news because you're in control of these things, and this book will allow you to start working on them right away. You will gain a proven, practical, and comprehensive framework for understanding the behaviors you can practice to build and sustain trust. We're going to help you pinpoint the actions that test trust, and we're going to reveal the steps you can take to rebuild trust when it's been damaged or broken.

Trust begins with you: with your attitudes, your intentions, and your behaviors within your relationships.

You don't need to wait on your boss, colleagues, or employees to lead the charge in building trust. You can take steps and reap the rewards of trustworthy relationships *right now*. Building trust (or repairing broken trust) takes energy, dedication, and self-awareness. But when you give your best efforts and diligence to the process, you'll benefit from increased energy, commitment, and confidence in your workplace relationships. We guarantee it.

The Need for Trust

When trust is present, there's a palpable buzz, a "can do" approach, and a belief that anything is possible. When people have confidence in one another's abilities, intentions, and commitment, they're more willing and able to participate, collaborate, and innovate. They are inspired. Trust may be intangible, yet the effects of its presence are concrete—both in people's lives and in the bottom-line results of an organization.

These results are crucial to surviving and thriving in a competitive, globalized marketplace. Every day, people are asked to work smarter, faster, and better. They're asked to do more with less, create new opportunities from epic failures, and engage in the steepest technological learning curve in the history of mankind. Trust plays a pivotal role in peoples' abilities to meet these expectations. In order to operate at their highest levels, people must trust one another and themselves.

You may not be used to thinking about trust as a primary driver of organizational culture and business success. But when you consider the everyday metrics that you use, you realize those "hard" numbers are all driven by the business conducted through human relationships. Business is built through relationships, and trust is the foundation of effective relationships. Trust is an aspect of the workplace that high performance cannot live without. When people trust one another, they open their hearts and minds to one another, forge productive partnerships, and collectively lower their shoulders to move mountains. Without trust, they withdraw, hoard their mental and physical resources, and search for the first available escape route.

Trust may be referred to as a "soft skill" by some, but we caution you not to underestimate its power—both when it's present and when it's absent. Building a trust-filled workplace is as vital to an organization's survival as piping in clean water. To stock a workplace with top-tier talent, attract powerful investments, and keep pace with an ever-changing business climate, we all must rely on thriving, trust-filled relationships. Without them, organizational spirits dehydrate and wither in the intense heat of a globalized marketplace.

Trust Is Tested

Trust is at play in every relationship we have—both at work and at home. In all relationships trust is built, broken, and made vulnerable. We've all been hurt, disappointed, and let down by others. And others have been let down and disappointed by us. Our trust is tested by the people we love, live with, and work with. And sometimes, our trust is tested by the very process of life itself.

While writing this third edition, we celebrated twenty-one years of marriage, milestones in our children's lives, and twenty-three years of business together.

Through those years, life has thrown us our fair share of curve balls and has tested our trust. Between the two of us, we've had three bouts of cancer: Dennis twice, Michelle once. We have lost both our fathers to cancer. And we have placed our faith in God that he would keep our youngest son, Will, safe while he served our country in Afghanistan.

We made sacrifices to support each other as we pursued our doctorates while raising two boys and starting our business. Our business has had periods of breakthrough growth and breakdown setbacks. We have experienced financial abundance and long periods of hardship. We have hired people who have come through for us while others took advantage of our good graces and betrayed us. We've had people tell us our work has changed their lives for the better, and we've had the wind knocked out of us when others have deceived us and taken credit for our research and work.

Our energies have soared through the presence of trust and have been depleted when it was broken. There have been periods when we were confident we could achieve anything and periods when we wondered if we were on the right course. Working through the pain of all these challenges, we have grown the fullest. Like many of you, we've learned firsthand that relationships take work and that trust is a must for relationships to be vibrant and long lasting.

More often than not, others don't mean to break your trust, and you don't mean to break theirs. And yet, trust is tested and broken on a daily basis as people do business together against tight deadlines, high expectations, and fierce competition. You let others down. They let you down. You're asked to support others, and you ask them to support you through these painful periods.

Trust is tested on a daily basis as people do business together against fierce competition.

Most people associate broken trust with big offenses—major acts such as lying, stealing, or manipulating others. Your inner voice may say, *I don't do those things.* And the likelihood is, you don't. Few people do. The hard truth is, trust is most often eroded by subtle, minor, unintentional acts that happen every day—*not* the big things.

Fred is late on his deliverable. Kelly delivers tough news and is shot down. Anna rolls her eyes. Henry gossips about Jane. Tony cancels the meeting for the third time. David won't talk about the "situation." There is the meeting after the meeting. This department points the finger at that department. Someone takes credit for someone else's work. You have to ask for the same deliverable or piece of information over and over again. Sound familiar?

We've found that 90 percent of behaviors that break trust in workplace relationships are small, subtle, and unintentional. You both experience them and contribute to them. You don't mean to behave in a way that breaks others' trust in you anymore than they do. You don't mean to disappoint them, hurt them, undermine their efforts, or overlook their contributions. But you do. We all do these things to one another. Trust is tested every day by the inherent messiness of business and human dynamics.

The problem is, these little, unintentional hurts and oversights build upon one another until you are forced to pay attention to them. When you reach this tipping point, you no longer just feel let down—you feel betrayed. You shift from questioning your trust to grabbing it back with both hands as quickly as possible. Feelings of betrayal resulting from the accumulation of small, daily breakdowns in trust are just as real—and just as damaging to relationships—as those caused by large, noticeable violations.

Ninety percent of behaviors that break trust in workplace relationships are small, subtle, and unintentional.

This is not easy news to hear. You may be bothered by the very word *betrayal*. It may represent a painful experience in your life you'd prefer to forget. Trust is highly complex, emotionally provocative, and it means different things to different people. It can take a long time to build and can be broken in an instant. You want trust in your workplace, on your team, and in your relationships. We will show you how to get it. In so doing, we will ask you to pause and consider your behavior and your approach to relationships. Trust begins with individual effort. It begins with you and your awareness of the fragility of trust in your relationships.

You don't mean to break others' trust. But you do. We all do.

Three Dimensions of Trust: The Three Cs of Trust

The solution to the vulnerability of trust is consistent, deliberate, trust building action. Practicing trust building behaviors signals to others—and yourself—that you and they are trustworthy. There is no shortcut to trust: it's achieved and maintained through visible consistency and alignment between what you *intend* to do and what you *actually* do. We've identified the Three Dimensions of Trust that are foundational to your trust building efforts and pinpointed the behaviors that build each dimension. We call these dimensions The Three Cs of Trust: Trust of Character, Trust of Communication, and Trust of Capability.

The Three Cs of Trust provide you with a common language and shared understanding of what *trust* means, so you can discuss trust-related issues with others and take action on them. As you explore each dimension, you'll learn specific trust building behaviors that, when practiced consistently, expand the level of trust in your relationships. Your trust in yourself and others will

Three Dimensions of Trust

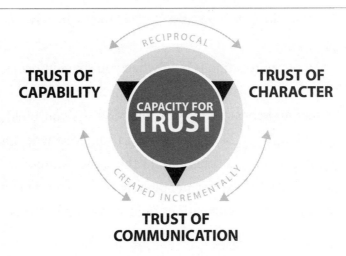

be increased, and you'll benefit from others' expanding trust in you: trust begets trust. The Three Cs of Trust are the foundation for your trust building activities.

> *There is no shortcut to trust: it's achieved*
> *only through consistent action.*

The first dimension of trust, Trust of Character, is the trust of mutually serving intentions and the starting point for all relationships. You build this dimension of trust when you manage expectations, establish boundaries, delegate appropriately, keep agreements, work the "win-win," and behave consistently. As you practice Trust of Character behaviors, you substantiate yourself as a generally trustworthy person who can be counted on—even in tough situations. Others learn that you do what you say you will do, that you establish healthy boundaries and expectations, and that you support them as they strive to learn, develop, and thrive in your organization. This is perhaps the most selfless form of trust, yet is rewarding to achieve. You know when you've arrived at a high level of Trust of Character when people in your organization start relating to you as a person they can rely on and depend upon.

Trust of Communication is built when you share information, tell the truth, admit mistakes, maintain confidentiality, give and take feedback, and speak with good purpose. As you build this dimension of trust, you become known as someone who speaks the truth and encourages others to do the same. Moreover, you become a trusted confidant as people realize you can be trusted to give and share key information—and know when it's ethical and appropriate to do either. As you learn to build Trust of Communication, you no longer engage in gossip or feed the rumor mill. You compassionately bring issues and concerns directly to the individual concerned. You work it out. You start to become the go-to "gut check" in your organization for people at all levels of responsibility.

The final dimension of trust, Trust of Capability, is most aligned with your unique competence. You build this dimension of trust when you acknowledge others' skills and abilities, express appreciation for work well done, involve others in making decisions, and encourage learning. At the highest level, Trust of Capability teaches others that they can trust you to know what you're doing, to ask for input when you don't, and to identify and develop the value that others could be adding to you and the organization. As you practice the behaviors that lead to high Trust of Capability, your confidence in your own innate talents grows, as well as your awareness of and comfort with your shortcomings. You become positioned as a resident expert, trusted subject matter coach, and a deeply competent professional.

The Three Cs of Trust are mutually reinforcing and reciprocal in nature. That is, as you begin practicing one set of behaviors, you notice that the other sets naturally develop. Additionally, you're rewarded as other people in your organization begin to pick up on and model how you manage expectations, communicate, and delegate. Trust begets trust.

Practicing The Three Cs of Trust behaviors lets others know they can trust your character, your word, and your abilities.

What Happens When Trust Is Broken

How do you respond when your trust has been broken? When you feel betrayed? Do you shut down? Check out? Pull back? Seek retaliation? Do you withdraw your spirit and energy from your work? Do you simmer and seethe? Simply go through the motions?

How do you respond when you learn that *you* have let someone down—either intentionally or unintentionally—and *they* feel betrayed? Do you defend, rationalize, or justify your behavior? Do you excuse it? Do you secretly think the other person overreacted? Or do you assume responsibility, reflect on why you chose to behave the way you did, apologize, and make amends?

When The Three Cs of Trust aren't practiced consistently, trust becomes vulnerable. Because you're human—and subject to the everyday pressures of life—it's understandable that you slip up and fall back into old patterns. Hurts, disappointments, letdowns, and breaches of trust are natural parts of relationships, including those with whom you spend the majority of your time. Even in high-functioning work environments and in healthy life relationships, trust can be vulnerable.

You let others down, and they let you down, either intentionally or unintentionally. We all know what it feels like to need to be forgiven. When you accept that you're human and embrace the fact that hurts, disappointments, and letdowns come with the territory of relationships, you're on the road to connecting with others on a deeper level. The key to unlocking your colleagues' passion, ingenuity, and commitment is not to expect perfect behavior from one another, but to have the tools, approach, and language in place to expedite healing when breakdowns do occur.

We all know what it feels like to need to be forgiven.

When trust breaks down, people tend to pull back and withdraw. They begin to question, *Is this the place for me? I thought I belonged here. Now I'm not so sure. I thought I had what it took. Maybe I was wrong.* They begin to lose confidence in their own skills and abilities. Some may go through the motions. Some do only barely enough to get by. Some become the "walking wounded." Others become victims. We hear the same story again and again as we work with clients: *My heart isn't in this place anymore* or *I just look out for myself* or *We've stopped thinking big and taking risks.* People of these low-trust companies report "a real loss in energy, passion, and creativity." When trust in a workplace remains broken and unaddressed, no one wins. Not organizations. Not teams. Not individuals. And not you.

Trust is a workplace's competitive advantage when it's present and its Achilles' heel when it's absent. As subtle instances of broken trust accumulate, people begin to feel betrayed—by their organizations, by their co-workers, and by their own responses to the situation. Their confidence, commitment, and energy diminish. Their ability to trust contracts. At a time when a competitive edge can collapse in days or weeks instead of months or years, no one can afford to ignore the role that trust plays in energizing—or destroying—meaningful productivity.

Trust is a workplace's competitive advantage when it's present and its Achilles' heel when it's absent.

You see the power of trust when it's present in your personal relationships—and the devastating impact when it's lacking. What happens when you find out your spouse has racked up thousands of dollars in credit card debt that you knew nothing about? What do you do when you discover that your friend has been hiding an addiction? How did your child respond when you were out of town on business for his birthday or missed her soccer game . . . *again*? What happened when your teenager lied to you about his whereabouts Saturday night? When a colleague took credit for your work? When your employee skimmed from the register? When you continue to treat your college-age kid like you did when he or she was in high school? When your boss gave vague direction about an important, time-sensitive initiative, then took off for a round of golf?

These experiences test the strength of your ability to trust others. When your trust has been breached or betrayed by a specific person, you can't help but call into question the entire relationship. You need to pay attention to broken trust and feelings of betrayal because not paying attention to them—and *not* dealing with them—comes at a cost to you. Betrayal creates a continuous leak of your energy. Eventually, the truth about how the betrayal has affected you will come out as your performance at work and quality of life at home suffers.

Broken trust—and the feelings of betrayal that occur when trust is repeatedly broken—is at the core of the human condition and is the heart of the struggle in human interactions. This means that betrayal offers a tremendous opportunity to pause your activity, reflect, listen, and learn. Betrayals can be gifts and teachers if we allow them to be. They serve as catalysts to assess your trustworthiness and strengthen your relationships. When your trust is tested or broken, you learn about the darkest corners of your soul and gain the opportunity to become a better version of yourself—both at work and at home. But that can happen only if you proactively engage the experience, acknowledge your own role in the breakdown, and integrate the lessons you learn into your future interactions.

Restoring trust is not a spontaneous process. It takes time, hard work, courage, and compassion, but the payoff is tremendous. We know this to be true because we've lived it for the past twenty-plus years. The most poignant example of our commitment to our specific, proven healing process occurred a year after the first edition of this book was published in 1999:

We were facing a crisis. Diagnosed with kidney cancer and hospitalized, Dennis had trusted Michelle to carry out their professional obligations on behalf of us both. Michelle reached out for help to a trusted colleague, who offered to step in and support a critical client project with a promise to deliver by the client's deadline. At the last minute, Michelle discovered her colleague did not deliver as promised and had failed to communicate her shortcoming. Michelle was left feeling confused, angry, and hurt by her colleague's behavior.

Michelle realized she needed to take action . . . fast. She fully acknowledged the situation, got the support she needed and an extension on the deadline, reframed the experience, and took responsibility for her role in the breakdown of communications before the deadline. Later, her colleague apologized and disclosed that her daughter had overdosed on drugs, and she had to take her to a treatment facility during the project's critical timeframe. She'd felt so ashamed that she felt like hiding, which she did. Once she was aware of the mitigating circumstances of the breakdown, Michelle readily and compassionately forgave her friend. She knew how challenging the situation had been because she had witnessed her own brother's fight with addiction. With Michelle's forgiveness, her colleague could begin to forgive herself.

You Have a Choice: Seven Steps for Healing

You want to have trust in your relationships. To have that trust, you need to be able to heal each time your trust is broken. Failing to do so will result in mounting frustration, doubt, and depleted energy. Our Seven Steps for Healing will provide you with a framework to not only recover from the deepest betrayals, but also restore your Capacity for Trust and work productively with those who betrayed you. These steps are more than a theoretical construct. They are a tested, proven, straightforward set of tools that work at individual, team, and organizational levels. As you acknowledge betrayal, allow your feelings to surface, get support, reframe your experience, take responsibility, forgive, and let go and move on, you free yourself from the shackles of doubt, fear, and destroyed confidence that betrayal can impose.

Seven Steps for Healing

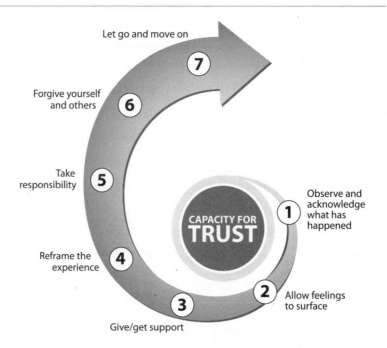

By utilizing our own Seven Steps for Healing, we were able to not only survive this experience, but learn from it, build strength into our relationships, and gain further confidence that the only way to approach betrayal is with compassion, intention, and courage. We knew that we couldn't avoid breakdowns in trust from happening again. Because we were equipped with the tools we needed to heal in the aftermath, we didn't need that security. We knew we'd be able to work through our hurt and disappointment constructively, and recover even more quickly the next time.

Transforming Your Culture of Trust: Transformative Trust

Building and sustaining trust can transform your workplace relationships into more than the sum of their parts. As you and your colleagues practice trust building behaviors with conviction, courageously acknowledge and address issues when trust is broken, and extend compassion and understanding to one another, you notice your efforts create an intense alchemy of broader organizational trust. You connect at a deeper level, trust one another more, and produce your best work. When trust reaches this critical threshold in your workplace, it expands exponentially, creating a new climate of caring fueled by a foundation of Transformative Trust.

The results speak for themselves in organizations rich in Transformative Trust. Suggestions for product and process improvements skyrocket. Productivity increases. Impressive results become the new standard and a source of organizational pride. Profitability follows suit, and everyone reaps the benefits of a thriving, exhilarating, compassionate workplace.

Everyone reaps the benefits of a thriving,
exhilarating, compassionate workplace.

In these high-trust work environments, you feel safe to talk about and share concerns without recriminations and to admit your fears. You feel secure enough to speak up about challenges and have the courage to ask for what you need to perform beyond expectations. And you feel empowered to willingly take risks, admit mistakes, and learn from them. You support your colleagues and know that you are in turn supported to go above and beyond in the pursuit of your organization's goals. A pervading sense of compassion establishes your organization's culture as not just an HR metric, but as a community filled with people who recognize, respect, and appreciate one another as human beings.

As you learn more about Transformative Trust, you're able to create a more trusting workplace through tapping your inner conviction, courage, compassion, and sense of community. You're seen, heard, and understood for who you are and what you contribute. Your skills, abilities, and knowledge are utilized and respected. Your co-workers have confidence in you and you have confidence in them. Moreover, you have confidence in yourself. You take pride in your work, your co-workers, and your company. Trust transforms you. Trust begins with you. The power is in your hands.

Taking Trust to the Next Level: The Four Pathways

Taking trust to the next level in your relationships and in your workplace means you must first strengthen the most important relationship you have—the one you hold with *you*. Your ability to trust others is directly rooted in your ability to trust yourself. When you enjoy a strong connection with *you*—with your physical body, your mind, and your spirit—you're more able to trust in yourself and extend your trust to others.

You deepen your Capacity for Trust through walking four pathways—Take Care of Yourself, Believe in Yourself, Make Room for Yourself, and Be a Friend to Yourself. Through these pathways, you learn to listen to the important signals your body is giving you about what it needs to be healthy. You learn to graciously accept and internalize the positive feedback you receive from others. You learn to claim the time and space you need to rejuvenate your mind and spirit. And you learn to extend the same kindnesses to yourself that you give so freely to those you most love and respect.

Through walking the four pathways, you deepen your connection with yourself and gain access to the energy, insight, and commitment you need to build, sustain, and transform trust in your relationships, both at work and at home. Trust begins with this connection. Trust begins with you.

Trust Building in Action

Reflecting on Your Experience

1. What extraordinary achievements have you seen made possible because people trusted one another?
2. How has betrayal affected your personal and professional aspirations? Can you identify any silver linings to these experiences?

Trust Tip ▶ *Business is conducted through relationships, and trust is the foundation of effective relationships. Trust builds the bridge between the business need for results and the human need for connection.*

CHAPTER TWO

Trust of Character

Introduction to The Three Dimensions of Trust

In the next three chapters, you're going to be introduced to the Three Dimensions of Trust, which we commonly refer to as The Three Cs of Trust, or simply The Three Cs: Trust of Character, Trust of Communication, and Trust of Capability. Together The Three Cs provide the understanding and practical behaviors you need to build and sustain trust in your relationships. Trust is inherently vulnerable. It means different things to different people and stirs provocative emotions in all of us. It's highly complex, yet is the baseline for how we relate to one another in one-on-one relationships, in teams, and across organizations. It takes time to build, yet can be broken in an instant. Subtle intricacies of human behavior create trust's vulnerability. To build trust into your relationships, you need a solution for overcoming its inherent fragility. The Three Cs give you this solution.

The Three Cs Solution

Your commitment to practicing the behaviors within each of The Three Cs will allow you to build sustainably trustworthy relationships. After all, you don't want trust just for today. You want it for today, tomorrow, and beyond. The Three Cs will empower you to build trust-based relationships that will weather the unavoidable storms of life.

Trust begins with you. We ask you to take the initiative to make The Three Cs your blueprint, and then watch as your behaviors inspire trust in how others relate to you. Trust building is not a spectator sport. Committed action, not empty words, builds trust in relationships between individuals, in and among teams, and within organizations. It takes courage to go first, to experiment with new ways of approaching your colleagues and practice behaviors that honor your intentions.

As you engage in the transformation trust building brings, remember to have compassion for yourself. We all trip up from time to time. You'll try again, and trust will grow. Let's begin your journey toward more trust-filled relationships with the first of The Three Cs Solution, Trust of Character.

The First of The Three Cs: Trust of Character

Dennis lay on the hospital operating table, about to undergo major surgery to remove a very aggressive kidney cancer. The lead surgeon turned to his assistant surgeon:

"Ready?" he asked.

"Ready," came the surgeon's reply.

Then, he turned to the attending nurses:

"Ready?" he asked.

"Ready," came the nurses' replies.

Finally, he turned to Dennis as he lay on the table, about to be put under anesthesia. The doctor asked if he was ready.

"One minute, please," Dennis said. "Can we take a moment to be mindful of this situation?"

"What? Don't you trust me?" the surgeon asked inquisitively.

"I realize this is a serious operation, and I have 'a lot of skin in this game.' I want to make sure this surgical team practices what we preach about trust—everyone is clear on expectations, aligned on purpose, working well together, and delivering as promised." Then Dennis asked the surgical team to join hands for an invocation before they removed his right kidney. At the end of the invocation, Dennis prayed, "May this operation be the smoothest, easiest, and cleanest."

Four and a half hours later in the recovery room, the chief surgeon told Dennis the invocation of trust must have worked. "I have been doing these operations for many years and this was the smoothest, easiest, and cleanest operation I have ever done. You lost only one cup of blood."

Trust of Character implies a mutual understanding between people that they'll hold true to their promises. That they'll do what they say they will do. You earn trust in your character when you keep agreements, honor intentions, and meet your own and others' expectations.

What Is Trust of Character?

Trust of Character is the baseline for trust in your relationships. It's foundational to your effectiveness at work and your trustworthiness as an individual. It opens the window to your inner spirit and intentions and lays the groundwork for connecting with others. The essence of who you are as a human being is brought to life through your character as you visibly demonstrate your intentions and commitment to "walking your talk"—or not.

You earn Trust of Character when you practice six behaviors: manage expectations, establish boundaries, delegate appropriately, encourage mutually serving intentions, keep agreements,

Three Dimensions of Trust

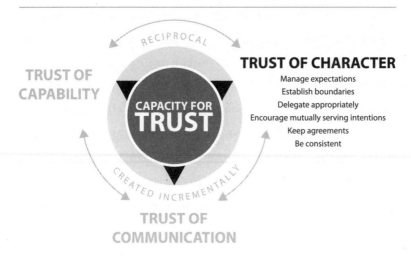

TRUST OF CAPABILITY

CAPACITY FOR TRUST

RECIPROCAL

CREATED INCREMENTALLY

TRUST OF CHARACTER

Manage expectations
Establish boundaries
Delegate appropriately
Encourage mutually serving intentions
Keep agreements
Be consistent

TRUST OF COMMUNICATION

and be consistent. When you model Trust of Character, you encourage others to do the same.

Key to Trust of Character is recognizing and honoring that other peoples' expectations, boundaries, and perspectives are as valid as your own. This is easier said than done. Pressures trump your empathy and compassion at times, just as others' burdens undermine their sensitivities toward you.

Have you put others in compromising positions by not delivering on your promises? Have you ever found yourself up against a wall when your colleagues didn't meet their commitments to you?

> *"The boss wants it done yesterday!" Gabrielle, a mid-level designer said in exasperation. "We have to get the product to market in two weeks, yet there are major problems with it. We know it will take longer than two weeks to get everything working properly. I don't know how many more fourteen-hour days we all can put in."*

Have you been frustrated because someone made an unreasonable request of you? Have you ever failed to ask for others' perspectives and put them in situations of having to achieve impossible goals?

We've all failed to take into consideration others' schedules, expectations, and peace of mind. And we've had our own needs overlooked. You don't mean to let people down, just as they don't mean to hurt you. Disappointment simply comes with the territory of human relationships. When these occasions persist, however, trust breaks down. You feel like "just another cog in the wheel" of others' agendas and the never-ending quest for faster deliverables. You stop taking risks, are unable to tap your creativity, begin looking for reasons to miss work, and perhaps even start looking for a position elsewhere.

The six Trust of Character behaviors are one part of The Three Cs Solution to these routine occasions of broken trust. Practicing these behaviors on a daily basis will allow you and your team to get on solid footing. They will provide points of reference for your engagement with others and help you create the trust-based environment you want and need. Trust begets trust. Trust begins with you.

Behaviors that Build Trust of Character

You want Trust of Character. You need it. You deserve it. You build it through being intentional in your daily behaviors, the first of which is managing expectations.

Manage Expectations

Trust of Character relies on managing expectations: your expectations of others, theirs of you, and yours of yourself. Expectations arise from needs. Individual, team, and organizational needs are at play daily. We all have needs and unique approaches to satisfying them or guiding others to do so. Some of those approaches are more effective than others in preserving and building trust in your relationships.

When your boss or colleague sets an expectation for you that's unrealistic and you aren't able to renegotiate the goal, trust is compromised. When you aren't given the resources and support you need to meet expectations, trust is damaged. You may feel set up to fail rather than to succeed. You test trust in yourself when you don't clearly state your needs or you don't equip others to meet your expectations. When people find themselves going through gyrations to understand needs or feel overwhelmed and under resourced, they struggle to meet expectations. Trust erodes, resentment brews, and results suffer.

**We test trust when we don't fully equip
others to meet our expectations.**

"My boss said I'd have access to R&D's research," Steve, a process engineer, told us. "But they don't seem to know what's going on over there, and I keep getting pushback. I'm never going to get this initiative off the ground without their help. Maybe my boss wasn't clear about what I needed. Or maybe he didn't even talk to them. Who knows? The problem is, he left town for a conference and isn't available to make anything happen until it is too late. He isn't happy when his deadlines aren't met, but it's his own fault."

Expectations go unmet for a variety of reasons. Sometimes, they've not been properly identified, explained, or clearly understood. Or maybe they've been understood, but they were unreasonable from the outset or inadequately supported. Unclear expectations cause misperceptions and misconstrued intentions, which interrupt trust in your relationships, both at work and at home. Even small instances of unmet obligations can lead to larger feelings of betrayal.

Be Explicit. To head off the confusion that can surround expectations, it's important that you're explicit in communicating your needs and in asking for detail about others' needs. Being explicit creates clarity, alignment, and synergy. Regardless of whether you plan to start a project, form a task force, develop a unit, or delegate the simplest of tasks, you build trust when you set clear direction for what you expect from your own and others' efforts and ask for clarity on expectations that have been set for you. Failing to practice either of these behaviors opens the door to frustration, and possibly even failure. Things become harder than they need to be.

> *Maria, a newer addition to the organization, was struggling to understand her boss's expectations. At the peak of her frustration, she asked her boss to lunch. During the informal meeting, Maria was very candid with her supervisor: "I told her that I just wasn't sure I understood what she wants from me. I told her I wanted to do good work, but I felt like I kept going down the wrong road." Maria had laid out what she thought her boss was looking for, and the two began to build clarity around the expectations of her position. "We went back and forth," Maria later told a colleague. "We explored a lot of options and talked about the breakdowns that had occurred. It was difficult at first to be so candid, but, after a short while, we got our creative juices flowing and I gained a lot of clarity for my role with the company."*

By allowing herself to be vulnerable and admit her confusion surrounding expectations directly to her boss, Maria demonstrated her commitment to contribute to her workplace in an impactful way. This commitment revealed Maria's strong Trust of Character, which encouraged her boss to trust her more fully. As the two worked collaboratively to define expectations, what began as a task-focused conversation transformed into deeper opportunities for Maria's professional development within the organization.

When you strive for clarity, you build collaboration into your relationships, even when expectations are high. Remember, you and your co-workers want to make a difference. You want to do your best work. Everybody wants and needs to know what is expected of them and wants others to understand their expectations. When you discuss goals and ensure everyone understands the related expectations, you open channels for support, and you contribute to business success and meaningful relationships.

How do you open dialogue to clarify expectations? On the next page we've listed sample questions and statements that can help you begin conversations around expectations with your co-workers.

Make the Implicit Explicit. An additional "curve ball" to managing expectations in your relationships is the fact that many expectations are implicit, meaning they are unspoken or undocumented. Have you ever taken a new approach to solving a problem at work only to be reprimanded for going off track? Have you felt that everyone but you understood the rules of engagement?

An organization's cultural norms and traditions influence implicit expectations—as do individual assumptions, informal agreements, and past experiences. Relationships are jeopardized when implicit expectations go unfulfilled, often because people

How to Clarify Expectations

Clarify others' expectations of you:

- "I'd like to understand what you need from me. What is your expectation?"
- "How do you want this to look? Do you have a picture in your head? What do you want to have accomplished?"
- "I'm not sure what you're looking for. May I have some direction?"
- "I want to do my best. I'd like to schedule some time to review your expectations and make sure I understand what you need from me."
- "Can I have a half hour of your time to make sure we're still aligned? I need some help securing the resources I need to meet the goals you've set for me. Will you help me with that?"
- "I've run into trouble, and I'm afraid I'm not going to be able to deliver by deadline. Can we talk about how to head off this breakdown?"
- "I'm having difficulty, and I may be off track or going down the wrong road. I'd like to check in with you."

Clarify your expectations of others:

- "I'd like to make sure I've done a good job establishing expectations. Please review with me your understanding of what I've asked you to do."
- "Are these expectations realistic? Do you see stumbling blocks that I haven't addressed?"
- "Is the timetable aligned with our standards of quality? Is it doable?"
- "Let's set up a time to meet next week and review what you've accomplished so far, and then make sure we're still aligned in our understanding of what is needed."
- "Is there anything that you sense might become an issue down the road?"
- "Before we say good-bye, I'd like to check in. Do you have what you need from me?"

discover needs they didn't realize they had until those needs weren't met.

Unfortunately, most of us don't identify implicit expectations until we've felt the consequences of not meeting them or experienced the disappointment when they weren't met by others. Have you ever realized you weren't clear about your expectations of others until your needs weren't met? In order to be proactive in spotting these unstated needs, reflect on your workplace relationships. Make a list of what you expect from yourself, and from your bosses, co-workers, and employees. Make a list of what you believe they expect from you.

Take inventory of where expectations are being met and where they aren't. Consider where you may not have been as clear as you could have been. What discussions do you need to revisit? Where do you need to clarify your expectations, and where do you need to seek clarification? You may discover that what you expect from others is similar to what they expect from you. Remember, you get what you give, and the surest way to gain Trust of Character is to give it.

Most of us don't identify implicit needs until they haven't been met.

Establish Boundaries

Jackie, an IT project lead, had been asked to collaborate with the accounting department, but she didn't know who did what. She kept getting the run-around when she tried to nail anyone down about it. "I've been trying to get information for two weeks," Jackie told Frank. "Each person I ask points the finger at someone else, who then passes the buck yet again. I'm about to just give up."

*Kevin's department was experiencing its third restruc-
ture in eighteen months. His head was spinning, and he went
to his boss for clarity: "I don't know what my role is. Can
you help me figure it out?" His boss just shook his head. "I
wish I could, Kevin," he said. "But I'm as confused as you
are. I don't understand the role of our team—or even our
purpose—anymore.*

Establishing boundaries around how work gets done takes the
guesswork out of knowing what individuals or team do what and
why they do it. When roles and responsibilities are clearly defined,
you know how you and others fit into teams and how those teams
fit into your organization. This clarity allows you to collaborate
smoothly because you know where to go with questions, for information, and with innovative ideas when they kick in.

Although some may contend that boundaries separate people,
they actually forge points of connection. When a team's purpose,
individual role, and responsibilities are anchored by clear boundaries, people are freed up to see points of connection where their
work intersects with that of their colleagues. The more defined
boundaries are, the more flexibly you and others can work across
them. You have the understanding and structure you need to participate in healthy and creative risk taking for the good of the
organization.

The less clear boundaries are, the more likely people are to
spend their time second-guessing their places on the team and
within the organization. In the end, they may opt to play it safe
and not risk crossing lines that may or may not actually exist.
Risk taking, creativity, innovation, and collaboration suffer when
boundaries are not adequately defined.

---

*Boundaries provide points of connection and
opportunities for collaboration.*

What can you do to clarify boundaries? You can reflect upon the goals and objectives you're responsible for accomplishing on a daily basis or in association with a project or initiative. You can think about the relationships you rely on in order to be effective. It may be helpful to identify where you are clear about your own and others' boundaries, to pinpoint where your understanding is vague, or where you simply don't know that boundaries lie.

You can also take a second look at your job description and job duties. Do they match the work you're actually doing? Generally speaking, job descriptions identify baseline expectations and should describe 50 to 75 percent of an individual's role. The rest of your work may require role flexibility as business needs arise and priorities shift. If you're seeking to advance in your organization, a career development conversation with your boss could prove beneficial in establishing the boundaries of your position and exploring how you're going above and beyond your current level of responsibility.

What can your team do to clarify boundaries? It's a trust building best practice for teams to devote time to discuss their purpose and team members' roles and responsibilities. Encourage your team to develop a team charter to clarify the team's purpose, objectives, and goals. Discuss the best ways for your teammates to work together most effectively to solve problems, avoid conflict, reduce stress, maintain productivity, and serve clients. Engaging your co-workers in establishing these boundaries instills a sense of common ownership and further builds trust in your organization.

Delegate Appropriately

"My team committed me to complete a marketplace analysis for our meeting with the senior leaders without talking to me first," Sara, a marketing specialist, said. "They have no idea how much time and effort this analysis will take. They simply handed it off to me. There is no one I can turn to for help. I'm scrambling, under a lot of pressure, and have to work late every night this week. I missed my little girl's dance recital, and she's upset with me about it. I don't blame her," Sara said with tears in her eyes.

You may associate delegation with assignments that are given out from the boss or leader of a project or initiative. This form of delegation is central to reporting relationships. Delegation also occurs informally between peers, however. When done appropriately, this form of delegation fosters collaboration and mutual support.

Delegation may take the shape and form of a "hand off" to a team member or a request for support from a colleague. Whether you're giving a formal assignment as the person in charge or handing something off to a co-worker, it's important to understand how to transition work effectively without falling into the traps of abdication or micromanagement, both of which erode trust in your relationships.

Effective delegation is giving responsibility to others and then providing the appropriate authority, resources, and ongoing support needed to fulfill your request. The process of delegation can be time and energy intensive as you strive to make sure those who you asked for support are fully equipped and empowered to give it. You delegate effectively when you build clarity into your expectations, define the boundaries within which the work should be completed, and set explicit, mutually agreed-upon measures of accountability. You develop Trust of Character by practicing meaningful delegation, by accepting and respecting your responsibility for ensuring that others are positioned to do what you ask them to do.

Know the Difference between Delegation and Abdication.

When you give people the responsibility to do a task or function but not the necessary authority, resources, and support to accomplish their goals, you've not delegated responsibility—you've abdicated it. Abdication removes the feedback mechanisms that allow people to voice their questions or concerns about how to accomplish their work. This lack of communication sets them up for lost productivity, stress, and possibly even failure. Although you may be intending to communicate your high level of trust in those to whom you assign responsibility, the degree to which you abdicate may end up breaking that trust rather than building it.

Recognize Micromanagement. Delegation requires a certain amount of letting go. You effectively delegate when you set the parameters and give the individual the opportunity to accomplish the task. When you delegate a task, then look over people's shoulders and tell them exactly how to do the work, you haven't delegated—you've micromanaged. You've given trust, then taken it away. You've sent a mixed message that erodes trust in your relationship: "I trust you, but not really." Have you felt your confidence slip when someone doesn't quite trust you to get the job done? The feeling sticks with you and influences how you bring yourself to your other relationships, including the one you have with yourself.

Delegation requires a certain amount of letting go.

To avoid the breakdowns in trust from abdication and micromanagement, it's a good practice to ask people if they have the guidance they need from you and room to carry out the assignment in their unique way. When the work begins, check back in to see if they have the information, resources, and tools they need to be effective. If not, help them get what they need. Establish explicit, mutually agreed-upon expectations for the task or project and set a schedule for status reports that you both create to communicate progress and new information. Create a two-way feedback loop to ensure continued mutual understanding and alignment. This "communication highway" will help both parties feel secure in the status of the project and feel good about the progress they make.

> *Linda, a project manager, oversees a major project in which her direct report, Ted, plays a role. She promised the client that the project would be on time and on budget. Linda reviewed the parameters three times with Ted and felt certain he understood them. Ted's part of the project, however, came in over budget and behind schedule. "Other things came up," Ted responded when Linda questioned his performance. Linda was furious. Ted betrayed her. She had given her word to the client, and now her word meant nothing.*
>
> *Linda and Ted sat down and talked about what contributed to the breakdown. Linda came to realize she had not delegated appropriately. She'd failed to establish periodic check-ins with Ted to ensure he was making appropriate progress to guarantee on-time, on-budget deliverables.*

Ted came to realize he dropped the ball when he didn't go to Linda and talk with her about the other work that came up. He did not let her know when he was struggling to balance the project's timeline with other demands.

Linda reassigned Ted the project. This time, they set up regular meetings to talk about progress, and Ted let Linda know what support he needed along the way. Linda took the first step. "I gave Ted another chance. I had a heart-to-heart talk with him. I reviewed my expectations and clarified his questions. I checked for his understanding by having him repeat back his grasp of his role and responsibilities. Then I asked for his agreement to the new expectations, with incremental goals at regular intervals. In validating the agreement, I shared the project's success with him."

Over the next six months, Ted and Linda's new strategy and consistent behavior began to pay off. Within a year, Ted proved to be one of the most reliable project engineers in the group. Trust was restored and strengthened and the organization as a whole benefitted, as others began to observe and model the dynamics of Ted and Linda's relationship.

Trust begins with you. As you delegate and accept new responsibility, you can take the steps that are needed to prevent letdowns, disappointments, frustrations, and broken trust. Delegation can be an occasion for excitement, high energy, and tremendous opportunity. It can open doors to learning about your organization, engaging with meaningful projects, or exploring talents you may not have known you even have. When you give away or take on responsibilities, you can discover new interests, instill confidence in others' development, and gain perspective about the mission and mechanics of your business. Artful delegation deepens your connection with others and develops your readiness to trust in both yourself and in your relationships. Trust begins with you.

Encourage Mutually Serving Intentions

You build trust in your relationships when you make sure your needs aren't the only ones you're trying to fulfill. When you think and act with others in mind and are interested in their welfare as much as your own, you create mutually serving, "win-win" outcomes. Work effort becomes fluid, trust is reinforced, and a sense of community is created.

> *Terry is a team leader in a finance department. He remembers how his team pulled together during a demanding time: "Our team worked really hard for months on a new financial reporting system. The timeline was aggressive. At the onset of the project, we gathered together and talked about what it was going to take to produce the outcome we all desired. We knew it would require a major effort to do a good job and that there would be personal sacrifices along the way. We also knew that this was a remarkable professional opportunity for us all. We all agreed that we would do what it took to deliver.*
>
> *Over the coming months we put in long hours—many late nights and weekends—and made personal sacrifices. Enthusiasm remained high because we looked out for and cared about one another. Although we knew we'd have to give up personal time, we backed up one another to make sure the sacrifices didn't come at too high a cost. On any given day,*

you'd hear how people were supporting one another to meet the goal without running their family lives into the ground: "Who has a kid's sporting event to get to tonight? I'll cover for you." "Did I hear it's your wife's birthday on Saturday? Take the evening off; I'll run the reports."

Operating with mutually serving intentions makes it easier to fulfill agreements with others. There are times, however, when your behavior may not serve the greater purpose of working for the "win-win." You may inadvertently leave someone out of a decision-making loop, fail to include all pertinent parties in the circulation of a report, or miss including someone in the invitation list to an off-site planning meeting. Under pressure, you may have an abrupt tone in your voice or speak in a demeaning manner. Such actions, though not intentional, cause others to feel hurt, angry, and even betrayed.

People's perceptions of your intentions—and your perceptions of theirs—influence decisions to trust or be suspicious. If you perceive that others' primary interests are focused on what's "in it for them" or in making themselves look good at all costs, you'll be reluctant to trust them. They'll have the same reservations about you if the tables are turned. Unfortunately, if trust is low, you may tend to move into protective mode. In a hypervigilant state, you may personalize everything, see risks in your dealings with everyone, and tend to cast yourself as the victim of others' harmful actions. This obviously makes getting the work of the organization completed much harder.

**You create mutually serving outcomes when
you think and act with others in mind.**

Often people step into situations with a focus on what they are going to *get* from them. They don't give equal thought to what they have to give. We're all familiar with the expression *What's in it for me?* It's appropriate to ask that question, but if that's the *only* question you ask, you're officially in the mode of taking and not giving. We ask you to consider what you hope to receive from relationships. What do you have to give? Do you give the time, energy, and effort you hope to receive in return?

Supporting others and operating with a sense of shared purpose in creating quality products, serving customers to the best of your abilities, and honoring the spirit of relationships builds Trust of Character. Remember, building trust is reciprocal. You have to give it to receive it. Trust begets trust.

Keep Agreements

When you do what you say you will do, you build trust. Others see you as reliable and dependable. They know they can count on you to "walk your talk." It's simple to say you'll always keep your agreements. It's much harder to actually practice this behavior in the hectic pace of everyday life. Busy schedules, shifting priorities, and finite time and energy are all real, legitimate obstacles that get in the way of doing what you say you will do. You're not alone. The only person who has never broken a commitment is the person who has never made one.

When you keep your promises, however, you feel good about yourself. It's energizing to instill confidence that you can be counted on to come through for others. It's empowering to build and nurture trust. In fact, keeping agreements is the Trust of Character behavior that offers the quickest traction for building trust in your workplace relationships. Follow-through on concrete action items sends the strong message that you have integrity by keeping your word. It also shows you genuinely care about others, and you're willing to momentarily put their needs ahead of your own.

But there's no getting around it: we all slip up and fail to deliver on promises. No one sets out to let others down, but we all do. When was the last time you missed a meeting because you were engrossed with other work? Missed a deadline because you were sick or stressed? Failed to deliver a piece of information because it honestly slipped your mind to follow through?

Occasional lapses in keeping agreements are unavoidable and, in and of themselves, may not compromise your trustworthiness. When people continually fail to follow through on promises, however, trust erodes. Their character is compromised, credibility is lost, and they're no longer considered reliable, trustworthy contributors in their workplace. Unfortunately, people tend to forget the promises that are kept and remember the promises that weren't.

You can be pretty hard on others when they fall short, but you're almost always harder on yourself. Judging behavior does not help build solutions, however. The best route to keeping agreements—and supporting others to do the same—is to check out what's getting in the way of their fulfillment and to speak up the moment you discover you can't honor an agreement.

Unexpected obstacles, failing to say no when you should, or being faced with the "crescendo effect" of an accumulation of mounting pressures threaten your ability to keep your promises. You and your colleagues want to deliver. You want to stretch and grow and learn and contribute. As pressure mounts, though, you wind up feeling vulnerable. You begin second-guessing yourself and create your own delays. The next thing you know, it's too late

---

How Does the "Crescendo Effect" Keep You from Keeping Your Agreements?

- Your professional demands and personal responsibilities collide.
- You serve on committees, spearhead initiatives, and assume mentoring responsibilities.
- You volunteer to coach your son's t-ball team, plan your father's seventieth birthday party, and help your brother relocate across the country.
- You face a mountain of commitments from all aspects of your life.
- You don't see how you can do everything you've committed to.
- Something has to give—either by default or by conscious choice.

---

to keep your agreements, and trust has been damaged or broken—both with others and with yourself.

Nobody wants to let others down or be seen as the person who doesn't keep promises. What's most important to managing trust is how you respond when it's threatened. Remember, trust begins with you taking responsibility for your behaviors in your relationships. Even when others may have contributed to your challenges, it's important not to point the finger or lay blame. Doing so will only further undermine your credibility and put a target on your back when you're the one to hold up progress in the future.

When you acknowledge at the earliest possible moment that you aren't able to keep the original agreement, own your role in the hold-up, and renegotiate deadlines or deliverables, you maintain and even build more trust. Developing Trust of Character in your relationships means that you acknowledge others are counting on you and that agreements matter. When you work closely and openly with your co-workers to develop, negotiate, and ultimately keep agreements—even in the midst of hardship—you co-create the very thing you want most: meaningful, trusting relationships built on understanding, compassion, and empathy.

Be Consistent

No matter how thoroughly and effectively you *talk* about trust, you can't actually *build* it without backing up that talk with visible, consistent action. You are only as trustworthy as your next behavior.

Would you consider yourself a consistent and predictable person? Do your daily (and hourly) actions match up with how you want to be seen? Others need to count on you and you on them. When you're not consistent in your behavior, others may see you as inauthentic or as a hypocrite with double standards. Inconsistent behavior raises questions: *How can I trust her when I don't know what she's going to do next? How can I know whether I'm going to get fair treatment or an honest performance evaluation? He shoots from the hip; I never know what he's going to say. Will I get the "nice" version or the "angry" version today?*

When your behavior is consistent, your co-workers aren't distracted, wondering which side of your personality they're going to experience that day. They're more likely to reach out to you and connect on a personal level. Your boss is less inclined to micromanage you, your employees are freed from wondering if you'll have their backs, and everyone is released from the stress of "walking on eggshells" when they need to interact with you. People know they can voice their honest opinions and give healthy pushback to your direction without fearing you'll "fly off the handle" in response.

Consistent behavior lifts your relationships to a higher level, instilling confidence and commitment and encouraging people to concentrate on the work itself rather than the confusion created by mixed signals. Creativity, increased energy, and collaboration result, and feelings of trust flourish.

Consistency in behavior becomes particularly important during times of transition. Adapting to the demands of a changing business landscape will be much easier and more fluid if you've already built a record of basing your behavior on principles and values, not expediency or your mood of the moment. When times are good and things go well, you may not notice how important consistency is to building trust. When times are bad, you'll realize it's absolutely vital. Your consistent behavior and the trust it breeds provide the foundation for your relationships to thrive when everything else is changing.

When your behavior is consistent, you are more likely to connect with people on a personal level.

The Journey toward Trust of Character

Manage expectations, establish boundaries, delegate appropriately, encourage mutually serving intentions, keep agreements, and be consistent: in this chapter, we've given you what you need to build Trust of Character in your relationships, both at work and at home. As you practice these behaviors in your daily interactions, we ask you to remember to have patience with yourself. Trust building is a process. There will be periods where you'll make great strides in shifting your behaviors toward those that build trust. Yet there will also be times when you'll struggle to incorporate all of the behaviors explored in this and in the following two chapters.

Our goal in providing insights into the behaviors that build The Three Cs of Trust is to help you become more aware of how you can show up differently in your relationships in order to attract greater trust. This is incremental work. Trust is built one thought, intention, and behavior at a time. We encourage you to have compassion for yourself and others as you seek to integrate these trust-building behaviors into your lives.

Trust Building in Action

Reflecting on Your Experience

1. Where in your personal and work life do you experience high levels of Trust of Character?

2. Review the six behaviors that contribute to Trust of Character. Choose one or two that you feel represent opportunities for you to work on increasing this dimension of trust in your relationships with others.
   - Manage expectations
   - Establish boundaries
   - Delegate appropriately
   - Encourage mutually serving intentions
   - Keep agreements
   - Be consistent

3. When you need to turn to someone for help, who do you think of first? Why do you trust this person? Now think of someone you don't trust. How do the two compare? What can you learn from this comparison?

Trust Tip ▶ *The business of relationships starts with Trust of Character—walking your talk, doing what you say you will do, expressing interest in others' well-being, and being consistent in your behaviors.*

CHAPTER THREE

Trust of Communication

The Second of The Three Cs: Trust of Communication

"I'm really disappointed and disturbed!" Laurie stated. "As a supervisor of this unit, I'm always looking out for my people and trying to do the right thing for the company. I can't believe my employees perceived my actions as self-serving!"

Have you ever felt the pain of being misunderstood? Have people misread your intentions as self-serving when you were honestly acting in the best interests of your company? Have you been in situations where others had negative perceptions that were far from the truth, yet they operated on those incorrect assumptions without checking their accuracy?

"All I did was inform the boss about what was happening out in the field—information he needed to know—and he blew up at me!" Bob, a new sales rep, said in exasperation. "I'm never going to stick my neck out again!"

Have you ever been shot down as the messenger communicating bad news, yet you had nothing to do with creating that bad news? Maybe you were trying to avert major problems, even head off a disaster for the company, yet your good intentions were neither acknowledged nor appreciated. Possibly you were even punished for being proactive.

Whether the situation involves relationships with your coworker, bosses, or employees, painful misunderstandings, illplaced outbursts, and undeserved hurts happen every day on the job. They result in decreased risk taking and collaboration, breakdowns in information sharing, diminished performance, and damaged Trust of Communication.

What Is Trust of Communication?

Trust of Communication is the form of trust that allows you and your colleagues to know where you stand with one another and with your shared work. It's the trust that creates an environment of openness and transparency that "greases the skids" for collaboration and candid two-way exchanges. It empowers you to

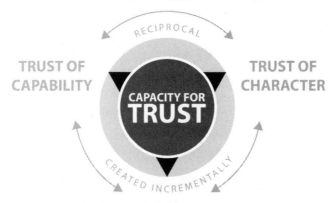

Three Dimensions of Trust

TRUST OF CAPABILITY

RECIPROCAL

CAPACITY FOR **TRUST**

TRUST OF CHARACTER

CREATED INCREMENTALLY

TRUST OF COMMUNICATION
Share information
Tell the truth
Admit mistakes
Give and receive constructive feedback
Maintain confidentiality
Speak with good purpose

both give and get the information you need to do your job, take responsibility for and learn from your mistakes, and talk through issues and concerns with an eye toward deep understanding and effective resolutions. Trust of Communication helps you create workplace relationships infused with positive energy, a sense of community, and shared purpose.

You earn Trust of Communication by practicing six primary behaviors: share information, tell the truth, admit mistakes, give and receive constructive feedback, maintain confidentiality, and speak with good purpose.

Behaviors that Contribute to Trust of Communication

You need Trust of Communication to develop open, honest interactions that will support you and your colleagues in doing your best work. You want trustworthy communication, right? Cultivating it begins with you. Let's explore how to get it by practicing the six Trust of Communication behaviors.

Share Information

Do the people you work with willingly provide information to others? Or is information shared on a "need to know" basis? Do *you* assume you're obligated to share only what others need to complete specific tasks or projects? Do your bosses or colleagues take this approach with you? Answering these questions requires honesty, both with yourself and with others.

Think about how fast the world is moving and how this speed highlights the importance of fluid information flow. You know firsthand how vital information is to you. You can't be effective without it. You and others need timely information to tie your efforts to your organization's purpose and strategy.

In theory, people know how important sharing information is. In practice, however, they all too often experience the burden of progress being interrupted when critical information isn't received. Trust of Communication breakdowns persist when you and others can't get your hands on the information you need to do your jobs. This is especially true when expectations are changing.

Jerry, the president of a large manufacturing operation, asked us to assist him in assessing the climate of his organization. The changes the company had made were not producing the desired results, and the president had a sense that there was some disconnect in the level of understanding among the employees regarding the change. Although the president felt the detachment, he wasn't sure how to address it.

When provided with a safe forum to talk, people shared their experiences regarding how the recent changes had been managed:

"There was lack of communication—and much miscommunication—regarding changes that were taking place. People felt lied to. Human Resources had to pick up the pieces after being left out of the decisions. Even if management didn't have the answers, they simply needed to say 'We don't know.' It appeared as though leadership was operating in a chaos mode."

"The information flow has dried up. The rumor mill and grapevine is our source of information. We never know how accurate it is. We feel as though we've been cut adrift and are floating aimlessly."

The president's sense that something was wrong proved to be correct. The lack of information had contributed to loss of

confidence and trust in the future direction of the company.
As a result, people no longer trusted what they heard and
felt less committed to the organization.

When information isn't shared—or there's a perception that it hasn't been shared—people feel left out, let down, and betrayed. This is especially true when there is shifting of strategic direction, roles, and reporting structures. When the flow of information is stymied, people feel cut off from the pulse of their workplace. They sense they haven't been trusted with the information they need to effectively perform and, in response, withhold their trust from others. Anxiety increases; energy is diverted from the work at hand. Guesswork and doubt take over, confidence and commitment erode, and relationships and results suffer. Positive outcomes are rare when needed information is withheld—even if that concealment is unintentional.

On the other hand, when information is shared, people develop the clarity they need to do their best work, extend information to others in good faith, and enjoy the blossoming of collaborative relationships. They feel safe to voice their perspectives, questions, and concerns, and navigate the impact of change on their lives. When you and others are armed with a sense of knowing what's what, you're able to focus on performing your jobs with confidence rather than expend energy trying to fill information gaps. You feel informed and connected, and you find comfort in knowing that whatever happens, you're in good company to weather the storm.

Sharing information inspires collaborative relationships.

Given the payoffs to sharing information, why would people withhold it? There are numerous reasons—some conscious, deliberate, and based on good reasons, and others not.

Information can be confidential. At times, managing information is a balancing act of keeping those with whom you work informed and fulfilling your obligations to maintain confidential and proprietary information. Transparency can be difficult in these situations, but not impossible. In these instances, it may be helpful to share that you're not at liberty to discuss some information, that you're constrained by a code of confidentiality. Then be clear about what information can and cannot be disclosed. Others will understand the need for confidentiality and respect your responsibility to maintain it. Your explicitness, genuine honesty, and commitment to maintaining two-way accountability will enhance others' trust in you.

Information can be a security blanket. In addition to confidentiality, personal insecurities may divert the flow of information, the most common being the fear of loss of control. People may fear that not being the only ones "in the know" will reduce their value to or power within the organization. This is most common when people are feeling particularly vulnerable and perhaps threatened. They respond out of a need to justify themselves and their roles. Or they may be driven to further their personal agendas or secure power or influence. You may find yourself withholding information for these reasons. You may not be ready to trust that others have your best interests at heart. The problem with this posture of gatekeeping is that you're inadvertently reinforcing a cycle of mistrust. When others see that you're withholding from them, they'll follow suit.

Information can be taken for granted. At other times, you may not even be aware you're withholding information. When under pressure, it's easy and normal to assume communication channels are flowing. You may not intentionally withhold it, but the impact of missing information on others is the same—diminished trust across your relationships, and perhaps even feelings of betrayal.

Trust begins with you. To avoid breakdowns in Trust of Communication, you may find it helpful to incorporate an information check-in with your co-workers, boss, and others who rely on you to provide them with updates. Review your understanding of their information needs and ask them if you're giving them what they require to do their best work. Expand the conversation by reviewing your information needs and extend the courtesy of asking for the most helpful method for you to give and ask for what's needed.

Giving and receiving information is in essence giving and receiving trust. Growing trust results in stronger work communities filled with people who know their peers will support them in meeting their goals.

---

*Giving and receiving information is in
essence giving and receiving trust.*

Tell the Truth

"I'm afraid of what will happen if I honestly share my thoughts," Roland, a quality engineer, said hesitantly. "I've developed a tendency to say what I think others want me to say rather than how I truly feel. This isn't the way I want to be, but this is how I feel safest in my current work environment. You'd think that as long as I'm professional and

*considerate in expressing my opinions, there shouldn't be any
negative consequences—but unfortunately this is not always
the case."*

Do you fear what will happen if you honestly share your
thoughts and feelings at work? Do you fall back on saying what
you think others want you to say rather than what you truly feel?
Do you ever signal to others—perhaps even unconsciously—that
you don't want their true opinions?

People need a safe work environment where they can voice
their concerns, feelings, and needs. They need to openly talk
about issues. People want straightforward communication from
their leaders and one another. This means no lying, no exaggerat-
ing, no stretching or omitting or spinning of the truth. Lying and
spinning destroy trust. If people don't tell the truth, trust can't
grow. This is particularly important in our increasingly globalized
economy, where honesty is essential to building trusting relationships cross-culturally. Because trust and honesty go together,
your ability to tell and encourage the truth is crucial for building trust and fostering honest communication in your workplace
relationships.

Your ability to tell the truth is essential for building trust.

It's important to realize there are different kinds of truth.
There is the truth about the status of a project. The status of a
decision. The status of change. The truth about a position. A client. A goal. And there are more personal truths—the truth of
your thoughts, opinions, and perspectives. The truth about your
confidences and vulnerabilities. Being aware of the different forms

truth takes—and being willing and ready to share all of them—deepens your trustworthiness in your relationships, both at home and at work.

Telling the truth isn't always as straightforward as it seems. People engage in half-truths or little white lies regularly. Have you been on the receiving end of a partial truth? A white lie? Experienced someone telling you what they think you want to hear rather than giving it to you straight? Have others been on the receiving end of you doing the same?

> *"We don't speak the truth at work," Julie, a schoolteacher, said. "People tend to withhold the truth or 'sugar-coat' it to protect the relationship or to avoid negative repercussions. We are afraid of the truth. We don't trust what others will do with it."*

Sometimes telling the truth can be difficult. You may be nervous others will get frustrated with you or won't like what you have to say. You may worry they will blame, judge, or criticize you. You worry that you will lose the relationship. You may not be sure if the person is open to hearing your perspective. You might slip into giving a comfortable variation of the truth—or sharing a partial truth—because you want to be accepted.

To help you come to terms with the inherent complexity of truth telling, it may be helpful for you to realize that the truth you are telling is "your truth." You are unique and the truth you tell is based upon your experience. Honor yourself and your perspective by avoiding exaggeration or putting a spin on your perspective.

Although you may feel safer *not* being honest in the moment, in the long run, your relationships will be damaged by this hesitancy. Avoiding the truth causes your credibility to break down, your trustworthiness to be compromised, and puts the acceptance

---

How to Tell the Truth

- State facts, and then offer your opinion or perspective of those facts.
- Be explicit that you're offering your interpretation of the facts, so there is no confusion about what you're communicating:
  - ▶ "This is my understanding of . . ."
  - ▶ "This is my opinion."
- Be open to hearing an alternate point of view:
  - ▶ "This is my take on the situation. What's yours?"
  - ▶ "This is how I see things. How do you see them?"
- Acknowledge that it might be difficult for others to hear what you have to say:
  - ▶ "I know this might be difficult to hear, but I'd like to share the full story . . . or provide all the information."
- Acknowledge when it's difficult for you to tell your truth:
  - ▶ "This is hard for me. I feel a bit awkward."
  - ▶ "I'm a little nervous how you or others might react."
- Check the accuracy and appropriateness of your information:
  - ▶ "This is the information I have. These are the facts, as I understand them. Have I missed something?"

---

you seek at risk. Hiding the truth fosters an environment of doubt and confusion where it's impossible for trust to grow. In the end, you don't feel good about yourself.

Telling the truth takes courage. The reward for having courageous conversations about your thoughts, feelings, and perspectives is that you're perceived as authentic and trustworthy. People notice your willingness to be vulnerable, and they share their vulnerability with you in return. As you extend trust through your truth, others are inclined to tell you their truth in return. This transparency will allow you and your co-workers to forge deeper connections, take pride in your work, make better decisions, and render stronger contributions to your workplace.

People often focus on the need for those in hierarchical positions of leadership to tell the truth. Yes, employees typically intuit when they are not getting the straight scoop. People working together side by side every day, however, are also highly attuned to receiving spin from one another. Truth telling begins with each and every individual. It begins with you.

Admit Mistakes

"When I take responsibility and admit my mistakes, it makes it safe for others to admit theirs," said Kate, a shift supervisor. "The last thing I need is to be blindsided by covered up mistakes my team members made that I should have known about and corrected before orders were shipped to our customers."

"We need to increase our speed to market," said Max, a project lead. "This means we've got to find new, innovative ways of manufacturing our products. I need everyone on my team to think out of the box, to take some risks. Yes, they'll make mistakes, but we all need to treat those mistakes as an investment in our future position in the marketplace."

As the complexity of the business world increases, it's difficult for you to have the right answers for all your questions and problems the first time around. You need to expand your approach and accept the reality that mistakes will be made along the way as you develop new solutions.

Your organization needs you to take risks in order to grow. You also need to take risks to grow as a person. Sometimes you'll get the results you thought you'd get and sometimes you won't. If you aren't making mistakes, however, you aren't growing. The biggest gains and deepest lessons learned come from mistakes— when you allow yourself to make them.

An environment where people take risks, innovate, and stretch themselves to make progress is an environment where mistakes happen. We all make mistakes. Even with the best intentions, there will be times when you are pulled in several directions or simply distracted by everyday concerns, and errors or slip-ups will happen.

How do you respond to mistakes you make? Do you beat yourself up? Are you hard on yourself? Or do you consider that you made your best effort? How do you handle mistakes made by others? Do you focus on the results they didn't get or search for insights and lessons?

An environment where people feel free to admit mistakes is an environment that inspires innovation.

How you respond to your own and others' mistakes sets the tone for your relationships and is a key factor in squashing or creating Trust of Communication. When you own your errors, you show others that you are a fallible human being, just like them. You show them that you care about your company, take your work seriously, and want to learn from your missteps. You let others know you can be trusted to take responsibility for your actions and that they can feel safe to do so, too.

Admitting mistakes isn't a sign of weakness—it's a sign of strength. You inspire trust. You become known as a person who suspends judgment, extends compassion, and gains perspective on why mistakes happened in the first place.

So, given the benefit of owning up, why would you *not* admit your mistake? You may be in a situation where you worry that you'll be judged, criticized, or seen as "less than" if you fess up that you messed up. You may be concerned that you'll be perceived as less valuable to your organization. Or you may be so overwhelmed with the pressures of everyday work that you're too anxious about how to handle your mistake. You might be tempted to "save yourself some trouble" by simply ignoring it or moving on as if nothing has happened.

Or, you might choose to make excuses or blame others.

The problem with blaming or pointing the finger at others is that you and they can't learn the valuable lessons mistakes bring. Thomas Edison tried 1,600 materials before he discovered the right one. You can choose to focus on his 1,599 mistakes, or not. Edison categorized his errors, learned from them, and invented the light bulb.

Covering up mistakes, justifying them, or blaming them on others wastes precious time, impacts productivity, arrests innovation, and stifles creativity. The impacts are equally negative when you put others down, judge them, or ridicule them for their mistakes: collaboration breaks down, trust is eroded, people pull back, and the status quo takes over. Remember, you don't break trust when you admit a mistake—you break trust in how you handle the aftermath of both your own and others' errors. Trust begins with you.

To admit your mistake, it's always a good idea to speak directly to those most impacted by your misstep. Taking responsibility for making corrections and forging a stronger path forward can go a long way in maintaining (or rebuilding) others' trust in you. And a simple "I'm sorry" is *always* appreciated, regardless of your mistake's size or impact. You can learn a great deal by reflecting on the perspective you've gained after the incident and considering how you can apply these lessons to your work as you move forward.

Give and Receive Constructive Feedback

"Many people here avoid giving feedback because they're afraid of confrontation or of hurting someone's feelings," shared Sylvia, an instructional designer. "Also, giving feedback can involve lengthy conversations where issues are brought to the table. Many times, it's easier to avoid doing this. I'm not saying this is effective, but it happens in this workplace."

"I know it's going to be difficult for Joseph to hear how he came across in the meeting with the division team," said Cliff, an account manager. "But I have a responsibility to provide him with that feedback so that he can grow from it. I don't want to rob him of that opportunity."

Do you avoid confrontation because you fear your criticism will hurt the other person's feelings? Can you open yourself up to receiving feedback—without getting defensive?

Feedback matters. Most people associate feedback with conversations that directly relate to job performance. It's true this kind of feedback is essential to trust building. People need to know how their performance is perceived. They want to know if they are on track, or not.

There's another form of feedback that builds trust, however: the feedback that helps you discover how others experience you in your relationships with them. This feedback is a powerful tool that helps you become more aware of how you're perceived by others. Sometimes, you show up in ways that don't match your intentions and you aren't even aware of it. The vast majority of behavior that breaks trust is unintentional. The only way you can become aware of your inadvertent missteps or the impact of your missteps is through feedback.

Giving and receiving constructive feedback is at the core of raising your self-awareness and building trust into your relationships. Through it, you and your co-workers learn how to create better work results, relate more effectively with one another, and add greater value to your organization and your individual careers. Remember, trust is the bridge between the business need for results and the human need for connection. Work is accomplished through relationships. You build trust when you engage in feedback with the spirit and intent to honor relationships and help yourself and others learn and grow.

Yet you may struggle with giving effective feedback. You may fear how others will react or be intimidated by their rank or level of responsibility. Perhaps you don't trust yourself to frame your comments without getting emotional, judgmental, or pulling unresolved issues into the conversation. Or you may work in a low-trust environment that positions feedback as punishment rather than as a learning opportunity.

Giving and receiving constructive feedback is at the core of raising your self-awareness.

Requesting feedback—and getting it—can be just as difficult as giving it. It's human nature to not want others to think you have shortcomings. It may be hard to hear that someone felt let down by you. Slighted by you. Or that your comment hurt their feelings.

Additionally, you may not trust what you hear because you have reason to believe the criticism is not intended for your benefit, but is rather meant to hurt or harm you. Or you may hear echoes of prior painful mistakes that cloud your perspective. And sometimes, it's just plain hard to look at yourself—or ask others to do so. It may feel easier to avoid conflict, shortcomings, and mistakes than be proactive in addressing them.

Hesitancy to give, ask for, and receive direct feedback is both understandable and common. Yet it can hold you and your teammates back from learning and growing.

> *Frank, a logistics coordinator, shared that his team meetings were too cordial. "Everyone is so courteous to one another— too courteous," he remarked. Upon our further probing, he detected unresolved conflicts among the team members.*
>
> *Because of their reluctance to confront issues openly and give one another constructive feedback, many issues simmered just beneath the surface of Frank's team and did not get addressed. Team members talked with their leader about their concerns, but they were unwilling to speak directly with one another. They hoped the team leader would intervene and do the talking. As the situation continued to decline, the level of trust among the team members deteriorated.*

No matter how difficult or uncomfortable it can be, it's imperative that you give, ask for, and receive honest feedback. Failure to do so robs you and others of chances to connect with one another on a more meaningful level and build trusting relationships. When perceptions are not shared and issues don't get resolved through constructive feedback, the issues of today get lumped together with the issues of yesterday. They grow in their magnitude and impact. Trust is undermined because people don't know where they stand or which direction to go next.

When others give you feedback, you may not always agree with what they perceive about you. It's important to remember that their perceptions matter; they impact how they bring themselves to your shared work. You may discover that when you keep an open mind, you learn something you didn't know about your-self, as well as about the people sharing their insights. Feedback helps you see things and create opportunities that otherwise may not have been open and available to you. This raised awareness helps you make better choices about how to improve aspects of your performance and move forward in your career.

> *Nicole is an office manager. In her small team of four peo-ple, Nicole served as the ringleader in pushing back against expectations set by upper management.*
>
> *"I don't mean to be disruptive, but I don't understand this new process," Nicole would interrupt. A co-worker observed how often she would self-sabotage her communications. "I think you're a nice person, but you don't know what you're talking about," she'd blurt out in a meeting. Her co-worker reread Nicole's emails and saw her efforts to engage. In every message, however, she counted the dozens of times Nicole had used the word but.*
>
> *"Nicole, you're the 'but' lady," her colleague Samantha shared over a cup of coffee in the empty conference room. At first, Nicole didn't believe her co-worker. Three hours later, Nicole came back to Samantha's office. She'd reviewed her own email correspondence and was shaken by her findings.*
>
> *"I'm so embarrassed," Nicole said. "No one has every approached me about this. I've always been told I am diffi-cult to approach, and now I see why."*
>
> *After receiving this feedback, Nicole began to speak her own truth with inclusive ands instead of exclusive buts.*

Evaluations, performance reviews, contract renewals, rene-gotiations, team meetings, and water cooler conversations: feed-back is part of organizational life. But how do you tell people their behaviors are negatively affecting performance or your working relationship? Important to remember is that it's not so much *what* you say, but *how* you say it—and the intention with which you offer your insights. Is your intent to put the person down, to prove him or her wrong, and to make yourself right? Or is your wish to make your colleague aware of how he or she is perceived and to strengthen the relationship?

It's not so much what you say as how and when you say it.

When you share your perspectives with a colleague, boss, or employee, it's vital that you keep the other person "whole." You do this by focusing on specific behaviors and being true to your positive intention to help rather than judge or criticize the other person's character. When people are put down or made to feel wrong or inferior as human beings, their human dignity is betrayed. No one wins.

When you extend compassion while giving feedback, however, you support others to see opportunities to improve something—whether it's a behavior, skill, or approach to a relationship. You demonstrate that you care for the other person and that you're willing to invest in your mutual effectiveness. You build a deeper sense of understanding for how to move forward together in a strong way. People feel safe in proactively requesting feedback from you if they trust your positive intentions in sharing it.

In addition to approaching feedback with compassion, you build trust in your relationships when you express your true thoughts and feelings in a timely and situational-appropriate manner. You inspire trust when you take the time to discover *why* they behaved the way they did and when you demonstrate appreciation and gratitude for your shared work and relationship.

You can reflect this gratitude by sharing what you appreciate about your co-workers and what you value about your connections with them. You may even wish to engage others in creative conversation where together you brainstorm ways you can strengthen your relationships. Do not underestimate the power of gratitude and appreciation. It helps to keep you, them, and the relationship whole.

To give feedback effectively, you need to be willing to receive it in return with gratitude. When others give you feedback, listen closely and hear their intentions, instead of pulling away with a focus on your comeback or response. Being defensive prevents you from learning. Make an effort to be open and show genuine interest in what you hear. When you do, people will experience your receptiveness and will feel safe in sharing their perceptions. You will earn their trust, and you'll gain the added benefit of hearing their perceptions again in the future.

Constructive feedback conversations take courage, ongoing discipline, and an expansive view of your workplace relationships. The traditional approach to feedback is top down—boss to subordinate. In trusting relationships, feedback is a 360-degree process, with all levels of responsibility respectively sharing their insights with their peers, bosses, employees, suppliers, and other external partners.

Having the courage to engage in constructive feedback conversations is an ongoing discipline that demonstrates commitment to fostering trust in your relationships. Consider engaging in feedback proactively to check in on the relationship rather than waiting for a disappointment or breakdown to occur. Share what works in your relationships, and then work through what doesn't on a regular basis. It may be helpful to explicitly ask what others need from you and be ready to share what you need from them to produce your best work.

> *In trusting relationships, feedback is a two-way street—you give it and you receive it.*

Engaging others to provide you with ongoing feedback demonstrates your commitment to your relationships and signals your willingness to accept help to continually grow as an individual. When this happens, the level of trust in your relationships is enhanced. Constructive feedback is a gift, both to those who give it and to those who receive it.

Maintain Confidentiality

"I'm appalled that my co-workers discuss confidential information inappropriately," said Nancy, a customer service representative. "The eagerness of some to expose confidential information about a colleague or misuse personal information of co-workers is demoralizing."

"If people come to me in confidence and share something that's happened to them, I honor their confidence," said Jack, a copy editor. "If I don't, I know rumors will get started, things will get out of hand, and damage will be done."

In any kind of relationship, confidentiality is essential to maintaining Trust of Communication. When others share private or sensitive information with you, they're demonstrating their trust in you. You have an obligation to honor their trust in the same way you would want them to honor yours.

You may link the behavior of maintaining confidentiality with critical, proprietary business information. The need for this kind of confidentiality is well understood and rarely violated. You know if you betray a confidence that is viewed as a business responsibility that you can jeopardize advancement opportunities or risk losing your job completely.

You are often exposed to other forms of information where confidentially is equally important. You may become aware of information regarding structure, roles, and responsibility shifts. Perhaps you become "in the know" of the creation of a new position, including the job's salary range. When this type of information is shared inappropriately, at the wrong time and in the wrong manner, it can feed the rumor mill and diminish the intended positive outcome of future announcements. Additionally, it prevents your co-workers from carrying out communications in a thoughtful manner and denies others the opportunity to hear news first directly from those who are tasked with delivering it.

When you share or become aware of key decisions and information via backroom channels and gossip, doubt and speculation often replace openness and receptivity. You and others may begin to withdraw and hold back from sharing your own information, for fear that your words may be misconstrued or used against you in the future. An environment in which confidences are not respected or maintained breeds distrust and causes damage to workplace relationships, perhaps irreparably so.

Do you respect others' requests to maintain the confidentiality of sensitive information? Have you ever slipped and let a secret out or leaked information to a close friend? Have you ever shared personal information that you're having troubles with your spouse, that your son is failing in school, or that you're looking for another job only to hear your private communication bounced around the water cooler a week later?

How do you deal with this kind of infraction?

Tips for Dealing with a Confidentiality Breach

The best way to deal with a breach is to have a direct, honest conversation with the person who leaked the information.

- Remind the other person of what you expected when you shared your thoughts:
  - ▶ "I trusted you with information. I asked you to maintain confidentiality."
- Be candid in your knowledge of what occurred:
  - ▶ "I've learned that you shared my information with someone else."
- Be explicit in your future expectations:
  - ▶ "I expect from you the same high degree of integrity and confidentiality that I bring to you."
- Ask for confirmation of understanding:
  - ▶ "If I have a conversation with you in confidence, I expect you to keep it in confidence. Are we in agreement?"

Having this kind of conversation lets people know that *you* know they've violated your trust. When you ask for accountability, it establishes a clear boundary and sets explicit expectations regarding future communications. If you fail to address breaches of confidentiality, then animosity and distrust will creep into your relationships with others. If this behavior proliferates in the workplace, its impact will destroy trust and cripple the organization.

Speak with Good Purpose

GOSSIP!!! Yes, I am aware of gossip around here," said Pete, a training instructor. "Who isn't? You'd either have to be deaf, dumb, and blind or living in seclusion not to hear it. Although I don't condone it, I'm sure I'm a perpetrator as well as a victim of it. When I gossip about someone else, I tend to feel guilty, but only after everything is said and done because, honestly, no one thinks about it when they are actually doing it!"

"We have an agreement on this team, to talk directly to one another when a problem arises rather than complain behind one another's back," said Theo, a mid-level team leader. "We've learned that when you hear others talking in a negative way, it's important to encourage them to stop and talk to the person directly. Also, before reacting to something you hear, it's important find out the whole story. Often what we hear through the grapevine is not accurate and can be quite damaging. Only we can stop that damage from occurring."

We've worked with hundreds of teams in different parts of the world. They all share a propensity to gossip. Gossip is the most frequent trust breaking behavior practiced in teams.

Do you talk or gossip about co-workers behind their backs? Do you share what is troubling you clearly and freely, or do you use insinuating remarks or slighting digs to convey your thoughts and feelings indirectly? When you're called to task for these belittling remarks, do you take responsibility or hide behind a white lie? *Oh, I was only joking. Don't be so sensitive!*

Have you ever been the brunt of gossip? Have you discovered that someone else's issue with you is the topic at lunch or after work drinks? How did you feel when this happened? What happened to your trust in others?

The behavior of speaking with good purpose is a litmus test for developing trust-based relationships. We've established that disappointments, frustrations, and trust breakdowns come with the territory of relationships. You speak with good purpose when you talk directly with the individual who has broken your trust with the positive intention of resolving your issues. In pursuing these straightforward communications, you establish your expectations that others will bring their concerns directly to you. After all, if people have issues with you, you want to hear about the issues directly from them rather than from someone else, right?

Gossip is the number one killer of communication trust in teams.

When you talk about your concerns with others rather than the person you have an issue with, you fuel gossip and feed the rumor mill. You contribute to a negative environment in which agitation and speculation steal focus from where it belongs—on the work itself. It becomes difficult for you and others to focus on goals and creative problem solving when you're constantly looking over your shoulder and wondering who is talking about you behind your back. Your energy is depleted by negative thoughts and concerns.

When you hide behind inappropriate humor and sarcasm, gossip, criticize, or shun others, you undermine trust in your communications. You shirk your responsibility to say what really needs to be said and inject negative thoughts into the minds of those around you—and into your own mind as well. In this way, you actually betray yourself. You not only lose trust with the individual with whom you have an issue or concern, but others note your behavior. They become sensitive to the way you speak to them and become more cautious with what they share with you because they don't consider you trustworthy. They may fear that you'll talk about them behind their backs, too. That fear is reasonable. If someone gossips to you about another person, you suspect

---

How to Speak with Good Purpose

- Prior to engaging with your colleague, take time to center yourself.
- Set a climate where you both feel safe to discuss your points of view.
- Begin the conversation by sharing your intentions.
- Ask the other party to give you more information about the concerns you have.
- Ask for your colleague's point of view to gain perspective.
- Assume the benefit of doubt.
- Extend compassion by withholding judgment and bias before you've heard your colleague explain his or her position.
- Be present in the conversation.

---

you, too, will be the topic of their gossip. What goes around comes around.

There are a variety of reasons why people struggle to find the courage to speak with good purpose: the most common of which is they just don't know how. Here, we can help.

Mounting, unaddressed issues that get funneled into the grapevine turn into major problems and conflicts later on—leading to devastating impact on your own and others' relationships, morale, performance, and trust. People's reputations and opportunities can be damaged due to gossip—not to mention the impact on the human spirit and work performance. The bottom line is that no value comes from gossip.

"Oh, but I was only venting," one individual shared to defend her gossip. "We all need to vent from time to time," exclaimed another. "This is how we connect with one another—we share our common concerns about someone else."

Everyone has a need to vent from time to time. When you use venting to help you gain perspective and prepare yourself to speak with good purpose, you preserve trust. If, however, you fall into the trap of venting without sound intent and responsible action, you've not contributed to a positive outcome. You've simply chosen to (wrongly) justify your gossip. Sometimes, it's easier and more comfortable to rationalize our behavior than it is to own it. When we take ourselves off the hook in this way, we betray trust.

Venting can easily turn into complaining, gossiping, and back-biting when it's not constructive. Although it may make you feel better in the moment because you've released your frustration, venting does not make the issue go away. There is no positive outcome unless you consider the steps you can take to work through your frustration, issue, need, or concern—directly with the individual with whom you have it.

Speaking with good purpose takes courage. Regardless of the size of the concern or issue, your ability to speak with good purpose, not engage in gossiping and backstabbing, and participate in courageous conversations will have a positive impact on your personal relationships. Others will notice the standard you set for yourself and be encouraged to follow suit.

As Alan, a savvy supervisor shared, "I have made my expectations clear: that people in this division address issues and concerns with one another directly rather than through a back door. To back up my expectations, I provided resources to help them develop the skills to do so mindfully. They now directly communicate problems and concerns to the appropriate individuals in an appropriate manner. Sure, there are slip-ups, and gossip does creep in. But it doesn't create the distraction and damage it once did. It is managed."

Speaking out against gossip builds a safe environment in which to trust. Be explicit in your relationships: Don't engage in gossip. Adopt a stance that backbiting behavior is inappropriate and unacceptable in your relationships. You and your co-workers will build trust as you stop getting distracted by the day-to-day drama of these "empty" communications.

Trust of Communication Builds Relationships

We all have a need for effective relationships with those we work with and live with. We have a need for connection with one another—to be heard, understood, supported, and given the benefit of the doubt—particularly when we trip up.

Trust of Communication nurtures the fundamental human need for healthy ways of relating and is essential to meeting business needs. Business is conducted through relationships, and trust is the foundation of effective relationships.

Trust of Communication is one thread in the delicate fabric of human relationships. This fabric takes time to weave and can become easily frayed or torn. Even a single conversation, including those that are misunderstood and unintentional, can have a significant impact toward building or breaking Trust of Communication.

Your credibility unfolds through developing trusting relationships based in meaningful dialogue. This connection allows you to find out what matters to other people around you. As you listen and respond to their thoughts and insights, you earn their trust. They feel comfortable to share more with you, and you gain a comprehensive picture of what's on their minds, as well as in their hearts and souls. You come to understand your colleagues as multidimensional *people* rather than as "the night shift" or "the finance department."

This realization allows you to develop strong relationships and gain others' support when you most need it. Inclusion and involvement become integral to your daily interactions. Your words and actions reinforce your trustworthiness. Trust develops between you and your co-workers as you understand they care for you and are there to support you to take risks and to fulfill your responsibilities. And you care for and are there to support them. Trust of Communication contributes to developing a safe and productive work environment where your Capacity for Trust in self and others increases, your relationships flourish, and your organization's performance expands.

Trust Building in Action
Reflecting on Your Experience

1. Where in your personal and work life do you experience high levels of Trust of Communication?

2. Of the six behaviors that contribute to communication trust, choose one or two that you feel represent opportunities for you to build more trust in your relationships with others.
   - Share information
   - Tell the truth
   - Admit mistakes
   - Give and receive constructive feedback
   - Maintain confidentiality
   - Speak with good purpose

3. How do you want to show up in your relationships?

Trust Tip ▶ *When you engage in gossip you are sending a message about yourself. You leave doubt in others people's minds about your trustworthiness. Their inner voice goes off: I wonder what this person says about me behind my back?*

CHAPTER FOUR

Trust of Capability

The Third of The Three Cs: Trust of Capability

"Why doesn't she just let me do my job?" Joyce, an event coordinator, asked in utter frustration. "It seems like every day, the boss is looking over my shoulder, telling me how to do my work. Why did she hire me in the first place, if she isn't going to use my expertise? Doesn't she have anything better to do?"

Have you ever felt micromanaged or underutilized because you weren't able to use your talents to do your job in the way you knew it needed to be done? Did you feel like your education and years of experience counted for nothing?

"I'm not very confident Sam can do this job." Abby, a programmer, confided to her colleague. "I don't think he has the knowledge or skills to pull his own weight in getting this project done on time and within budget. His lackluster performance since joining this company has me very concerned. We have a lot riding on this project's success."

Have you ever felt concerned about the capability of a co-worker? Do you trust the people who pass work to you or those who take on the next leg of your projects? Do you think they'll build on your good effort or screw it up and make you look bad?

These concerns and frustrations happen every day on the job. They whittle away at your ability to trust your own and others' skills and abilities and diminish performance across your organization. In this chapter, we'll show you how to build and sustain Trust of Capability in your relationships, and regain the productivity and job satisfaction you desire.

What Is Trust of Capability?

When you think of competence in your workplace, you may think of the formal tools used to measure and improve job performance: personnel policies aimed at tracking how well people do their jobs and formal training programs designed to teach them what they need to know. But competence on the job is more than education and training programs; it's more than hiring and promotion policies; and it's more than information, tools, and technology.

People trust in your capability when they have confidence in your competence to manage the demands and expectations placed on you by others—by your bosses, colleagues, employees, and customers. It takes more than task-specific skill to meet these demands: you also need to have the attitude, interest, and confidence that will help you work well with others.

Those "others" are an increasingly dynamic population of people from all ranks, levels of responsibility, and types of affiliation in your team and organization. As you work across boundaries and draw upon others' capabilities on a day-to-day basis, you need to be able to trust that these relationships will produce the results for which you are individually and collectively responsible. You need to trust in others' capabilities, and you need them to trust in yours. Trust of Capability infuses confidence in your effort and the outcomes it produces.

You know Trust of Capability when you experience it. You can see it, feel it, and hear it. People jump in to both answer questions and ask them. They don't micromanage or disappear when help is needed. They move with confidence in meeting their objectives because they know collectively they have what it takes to get the job done—today and tomorrow. They want to work to their potential and feel confident that others do, too.

---

*We all want to know that we are contributing
to the success of our workplaces.*

Trust of Capability goes beyond confidence in your own and others' current capabilities, however: it extends to having faith in your future potential to grow, learn, and develop. Do others believe you can take your skills, knowledge, and talents to the next level? Have you seen promise in someone else before he or she saw it in themselves? Has someone trusted in your potential and helped you to blossom? These are the questions at the heart of Trust of Capability.

We all want to be "seen"—to be recognized for what we have to offer and the value we bring to relationships within the organization we serve. We all want to know we're contributing to the success of our workplaces—that our abilities make a difference. In practicing the Trust of Capability behaviors, people are able to work together to harness and leverage that need and motivation, and create a place to show up and do their best work.

*When Michelle graduated from college, she went to work for
the Southland Corporation, the global chain of 7-Eleven food*

stores. She was hired into the company's management development program, which was designed to get people ready to run store operations. Once she completed classroom training, she went to work as a store clerk to learn the basics of managing a store—everything from inventory tracking, managing money, merchandising, and running promotions, to mopping the floors, stocking shelves, and scheduling staff. After working as a store clerk for three months, she was given her own store to manage. It was a 24/7 operation.

Michelle managed that store for three months and then moved into the position of area supervisor, which held her responsible for eight stores. She was twenty-two years old at the time. She ran those eight stores for a year and a half, and then was given a new group of eight stores, which she ran for nine months. And then she was given another group of eight stores, which she ran for close to a year. After proving herself as a competent area manager, Michelle was promoted to sales manager, and then district manager—a position responsible for running thirty-six stores and implementing corporate sales, marketing, and merchandising programs at the local level.

Just as she was finding her way in that level of management, Michelle was asked to take over another district that was struggling. This district consisted of thirty-eight stores that also had gas stations. It was the third-largest revenue-producing district of stores in the eastern United States, but it was not making money. Michelle had been identified for her ability to turn around failing operations, and she stepped into the job with a $40M budget and 350 people working for her. She was only one of two women at that level of responsibility—and the youngest and least tenured. At twenty-seven, she was seen as a shining star.

Michelle's rapid progression might give you the impression that she was a master operator. The truth is, she was not. In fact, in a couple of cases, she was promoted beyond her operational knowledge and, in some ways, beyond what she was really ready for. There were times when she was nervous, vulnerable, and worried about whether she could "pull it off." The operations were complex. She was young and still rather inexperienced. Reflecting back, Michelle believes the reason she was able to handle this level of responsibility so quickly was that she learned how to connect and build trusting relationships with others, and, in turn, trust in their capabilities.

The operations Michelle ran were outside of Washington, D.C.—a cultural melting pot. People who worked in her stores were from all over the world. She took an interest in them. She learned about their lives, their families, their hopes and dreams. She learned about their knowledge of store operations. And she asked them to teach her what they knew.

The company taught Michelle procedures and standards. She knew about gross profit margin and what she needed to bring to the bottom line: profits. She tapped into the people who worked for her to learn how to make that goal a reality. When she left 7-Eleven, her group of thirty-eight stores was one of the strongest performing in the region. She was being groomed for the next level.

Michelle received the gift of Trust of Capability—in capabilities that she didn't even know she had. This trust from others allowed her to develop a kernel of self-trust, which gave her the confidence to reach out and ask people for help when she needed it. She extended trust in others' capabilities and allowed herself to be taught by them. As she reached out, she discovered additional capabilities that allowed her to be successful beyond the limits of her defined skills and responsibilities. By giving her the freedom and flexibility to do her work *her* way, Michelle's bosses increased her motivation and ability to perform beyond expectations.

Trust of Capability is required to get any work done, whether that work is a specific task or a more complex combination of activities. People need confidence in one another's skills, abilities, and judgment to collaborate and perform at their best. When this confidence is missing, then expectations are not met, communications break down, and performance declines. Results suffer, as does morale and motivation. What can you do to head off these breakdowns by building and maintaining Trust of Capability in your workplace?

Four behaviors build and maintain your own and others' Trust of Capability: acknowledge people's skills and abilities, allow people to make decisions, involve others and seek their input, and help people learn skills. When you practice these behaviors up,

Three Dimensions of Trust

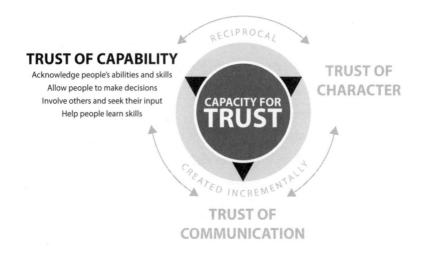

TRUST OF CAPABILITY
Acknowledge people's abilities and skills
Allow people to make decisions
Involve others and seek their input
Help people learn skills

RECIPROCAL

CAPACITY FOR
TRUST

TRUST OF
CHARACTER

CREATED INCREMENTALLY

TRUST OF
COMMUNICATION

down, and across your reporting relationships, you notice that others respond to your confidence in them, and they reach out to you for your expertise and support.

Behaviors that Contribute to Trust of Capability

You want others to trust that you know what you're doing. And you want to be able to trust them in return. To earn this Trust of Capability, you need practice the four core behaviors that show others (and yourself) that you can be counted on to be trustworthy regarding your own and others' abilities. Let's look at each behavior in more detail.

Acknowledge People's Skills and Abilities

> *"I have a lot of experience in this job, and one of the hardest things for me to do is to step back and let someone else do something," said Joe, a pipe fitter. "It's easier to just do the job myself than to guide someone through it correctly. Sometimes, I have to just step back and let other people struggle through as they learn to do the job their way."*

Do you acknowledge your colleagues' abilities to do their jobs? Do you allow them the freedom and flexibility to learn and support them to discover their own approaches to doing good work?

When you acknowledge people's skills and abilities, you're letting them know you see what they have to offer and that you respect their abilities. You provide them with opportunities to use their talents and develop new ones. Most people want to engage with their workplaces in meaningful ways, to invest their time and energy toward measurable successes. You build Trust of Capability into your relationships when you support people to make a difference.

Extending gratitude to your co-workers for their contributions, giving one another the latitude to do the work they are delegated to do, and spotting opportunities for them to grow professionally are key ways to build Trust of Capability. Not only do you grow trust in your relationships through these actions, but you contribute to others' capacities to trust in themselves. When people know they have your support, they're empowered to learn new tasks, handle new situations, and view uncertainty through the lens of adventure rather than fear or doubt.

You build Trust of Capability when you extend gratitude to your co-workers.

An added bonus to extending trust in your co-workers' capabilities is that as they're encouraged to grow and develop so are you. When your colleagues and employees assume additional responsibilities, you're often freed up to take on new projects, initiatives, and roles that you wouldn't have had the time or energy to tackle earlier. You also develop trust in yourself as a thoughtful, caring mentor—a level of self-trust that influences how confidently you engage in your own work and relate to others.

Anton, a developer, had an employee Margaret who was her own worst critic. She was so afraid of making mistakes that she couldn't take risks—even smart, necessary ones. When she did take a step forward and happened to make a mistake, she would repeatedly beat up on herself. Margaret didn't want to let the team down, yet her fear of letting the team down paralyzed her. She was so focused on her fear that she trusted the fear instead of trusting herself, and she continued to fail.

Anton took Margaret aside and asked if he could coach her. Margaret reluctantly accepted his offer. "I urged her to stay in the present," Anton said, "and to focus on the objectives, not on the obstacles. I encouraged her to reach out and ask for the help of her teammates." As Margaret began to focus on the task at hand and ask for the help she needed, she started to make some progress. Although she suffered a few setbacks, she started to trust herself and her teammates more.

Ultimately, Margaret was successful in accomplishing one major task, and then another and another. She started to gain a sense of success, and then pride in following through and accomplishing her goals. That was more than a year ago. Today, Margaret continues to grow, learning more about herself and developing deeper trust in her abilities as time goes on.

Anton often reflects on what he learned in coaching Margaret and how the experience allowed him to take the next step toward the position he wanted. Before Margaret, he wasn't sure if he was ready for such a big promotion, but once he'd seen that he could be effective in helping others achieve their potential, he had the guts to apply for the position. Later, after he'd landed the job, Anton reflected on his experience with a colleague: "Sometimes," Anton said, "another person's trust in us gives us the courage we need to trust ourselves."

We all have insecurities, doubts, and vulnerabilities as we stretch and grow. This is natural and healthy. It's not a bad thing to question your own and others' abilities to perform; there are times when you honestly don't think you or they have what it takes to get the job done.

Situations That Can Cause You to Doubt Your Own or Others' Capabilities

- You've taken on a project that's much larger in scale than anything you've previously experienced. The old rules don't seem to apply.
- You're using your proven talents in new ways, and you're hitting stumbling blocks in implementing what you know to be "best" practices.
- You're using a newly acquired skill or a newly developed talent for the first time.
- You're not sure about what you don't know, and you fear you may not find out that something is missing or you are doing something wrong until it's too late to fix it.

The key to moving forward when you have reservations is to reach out and ask for what you need, or find out more about what others need, to gain confidence. This act of reaching out will build Trust of Capability into your relationships. When others see you're willing to ask questions rather than blindly make assumptions and risk deliverables, they're more likely to trust you in the future. You gain their support and confidence. You become more confident in yourself to take risks and navigate challenging situations, and you become more likely to see the potential of others to overcome similar obstacles. Trust begets trust, and trust begins with you.

Allow People to Make Decisions

Organizational charts can't be described in hierarchal terms anymore; the days of two-dimensional, top-down models for management are gone. In their place, people are benefiting from working relationships and teams that span rank, level of responsibility, and area of focus. Lines of accountability have been redrawn to accommodate these new environments, where people are encouraged to address issues, solve problems, generate new ideas, and ask for help when they need it. To be effective in such settings, people need to be able to trust one another to make good decisions to move their shared work forward.

Do you allow your co-workers the freedom and flexibility to make decisions? Do you give them latitude and discretion on matters that impact their work? Do you respect the experience, knowledge, and judgment that go into their decisions—particularly in their areas of expertise? Do you support them in the implementation of their ideas?

Or, do you second-guess, overanalyze, and thoroughly scrutinize others' judgments? Do you fail to support the execution of their choices?

Sophia, an analyst, was given the sole responsibility to research the best options for launching a new line of business her company was planning. After nine months of extensive research, hard work, and due diligence, Sophia came up with three viable options. Her boss, Bill, took her work to the senior leadership team for review, excluding her from the meeting, and her ability to present her comprehensive findings. The senior leadership team took a mere five minutes to hear Bill's review of Sophia's findings, then quickly dismissed them. When Sophia heard the news, she was exasperated and deflated. "That's the last time I am going to work that hard, for so long, and give my blood, sweat, and tears to this company. What was the point, just to be so promptly dismissed!"

When you aren't allowed to contribute to final decisions that impact you and your work, or are contained within the scope of your assigned responsibilities, you feel devalued and disempowered. You may lose motivation to collaborate or contribute, and you might even begin to question your ongoing role in your team, department, or organization. You lose your sense of ownership and motivation for your work.

These same feelings are felt in others when you don't allow them to make decisions related to their responsibilities. They feel devalued and begin to doubt themselves and their approach to their work. As a result, they question your intentions and will most likely take a defensive stance toward *your* future decisions. When you don't extend trust and allow others to make decisions, you paint a big red target on your back for grievances about *your* choices.

When you aren't allowed to contribute to decisions that impact you and your work, you feel devalued and disempowered.

On the other hand, when you trust your co-workers' abilities to make good decisions, you reinforce their trust in themselves, and you encourage them to trust your decisions as well. This exchange of Trust of Capability infuses your workplace with optimism, energy, and a collective sense that individual expertise is valued. You lift yourself and others out of the mindset of doubting, second-guessing, scrutinizing, and fear. You open up opportunities for breakthrough innovation, process improvements, and enhanced profitability. You discover you are capable of more than you imagined.

You may encounter situations where lack of experience—either your own or someone else's—influences your willingness to support a colleague's decision. This is often true in a new relationship, collaboration with new partners, or when you start a new project and the stakes are high. It's important to understand the difference between appropriate trust and blind trust—and not fall victim to the latter. There are times when it is appropriate to involve others in a key decision.

> *"I allow people to make decisions when they demonstrate good judgment, aren't uncomfortable asking for help when they need it, and are willing to give help as part of a team effort," said Francois, a designer. "If I have doubts or concerns, I tend to be very watchful and offer assistance. I'm also proactive in being approachable, so they won't feel uncomfortable to ask a question."*

When you extend trust and allow others to make decisions within the scope of their responsibilities—and don't encumber them with micromanagement—you're doing your part to create an empowered, productive, *competitive* workforce for your organization. The extension of this trust doesn't mean you can't ask questions, develop an opinion on core competency, and offer support or advice as a project moves forward. On the contrary, these actions form the basis of the Trust of Character behavior of delegating effectively. The idea isn't to remove yourself from the decision-making process entirely, but to make sure the role you play in it generates trust in your working relationships.

Involve Others and Seek Their Input

> *Megan, an accomplished professional, was stepping into a new job. It was a big move up with lots of added responsibility. When asked about the first steps she planned on taking, Megan replied, "I'm going to spend a lot of time with my team and have them teach me what they know. I'm bringing myself*

in with humility and the understanding that I have a lot to learn. Yes, I'm there to lead, but I need to be open to hearing what others have to say if I'm going to be successful."

Can you think of an occasion when someone asked for your advice or opinion? How did it feel? Pretty good? Now, think about how often you invite your co-workers to discuss options, give feedback, and help you solve problems. Considering how much you yourself like being consulted, are you surprised you don't seek others' input more often?

When you involve others and seek their advice in brainstorming, problem solving, or work project discussions, you demonstrate trust in their expertise. When people feel trusted, they are more likely to take ownership of—and feel pride in—a project's outcomes. These feelings of pride inspire feelings of validation, which in turn cultivate your co-workers' trusting approach to providing input the next time you ask for it. When you extend trust and ask others for their opinions, you not only gain perspective and knowledge about how to do your best work, you also gain their commitment to your project's success. Ultimately, you do your part to create a more trusting workplace for both yourself and your colleagues.

A crucial warning: asking for input can't just be "lip service." The only thing worse than not being asked for your opinion is being asked, then having your thoughts, ideas, or concerns discounted or held against you in the future. These situations can lead to feelings of betrayal, as you or others suspect that your involvement was sought only to fulfill a line item on a checklist. The result may be that you don't feel safe enough to participate in critical discussions of problems or confident enough to ask for others' feedback when you really need it.

> ## How to Avoid "Lip Service" When
> ## You Seek Others' Opinions
>
> - Document what others share with you.
> - Thank them for their input.
> - Prioritize addressing the ideas, suggestions, or criticisms you receive.
> - If you can't (or choose not to) make changes based on others' input, let them know why in a timely manner.

Trust of Capability is built on the confidence in your own and others' individual contributions to the workplace. When that confidence is fed, so is trust. With trust, you and your co-workers are able to engage one another in meaningful, respectful dialogue and explore possible alternatives to shared challenges. You feel safe to question one another's assumptions in appropriate ways; secure in the knowledge that one person's new idea doesn't have to mean loss of power or authority for anyone else. The end result is an environment rich in Trust of Capability—one that ensures the full contribution of each colleague according to his or her talents, experience, and creativity.

Help People Learn Skills

"I need to know where a person's skills lie to make me feel confident in delegating a task," said Erik, a project manager. "So I talk with people before I delegate to see if they have the experience needed or if the task will require them to develop new skills. This helps me to know the type of support they need. It's extra work on my part, but the look on people's faces when they've learned new skills is priceless."

Do you take time to discover how you can help others do their best work? Do you take risks and tackle new ways of doing things, learn new skills—and encourage others to do so, too?

Investing in your co-workers' development is a powerful way to build Trust of Capability into your relationships with them. When you help your colleagues learn new skills, you demonstrate your trust in their potential and their ability to become the best versions of themselves. You create the space where they can discover what they're capable of achieving. And you build Trust of Capability across the organization as others see that you're committed to your colleagues' success.

When you help others learn new skills, you demonstrate your trust in their potential.

The pace of today's work can make it hard to find time to encourage others (and yourself) to learn new skills or develop existing talents. Staying "current" can take a lot of your time and energy, leaving little in reserve for "extra" work—even if that extra effort would pay off in the long run. Finding the time to encourage your co-workers to stretch and grow may be difficult, but it's a habit that, when developed, pays off in performance and creative problem solving—possibly in *your* next big project. When you and your colleagues are better equipped to do your jobs well, your results, job satisfaction, and competitive edge more than compensate for the time you invested in professional development. You grow as individuals. You grow as a team.

You can't afford *not* to make time for training that helps you develop. You have a responsibility to yourself to stay on top of your game.

You want to work in an organization that offers a wide array of training programs, workshops, conferences, and learning opportunities to observe others' methods and practices. You'd like to encourage and enable others to continue their formal education, take on special projects, or step into promotions that would further develop their skills and experience. But these opportunities aren't always immediately available—or available at all—due to funding, the size of your organization, or the sophistication of your co-workers' current skill sets.

Even if these formal mechanisms for professional development aren't available, don't forget your strongest asset for deeper learning: those *within* your organization with long tenure, proven expertise, and invaluable perspective. When you recognize and tap into these rich sources of mentoring and coaching, you not only learn from their proficiency and longevity, you engage a group of people who may have been feeling discounted or irrelevant. Your colleagues at the top of their career ladders have a wealth of technical and organizational knowledge that can rival formal professional development tools. Forging bonds with them can help you cultivate your own and others' capabilities—and build additional trust into your relationships as they respond to your respect for their lives' work.

Developing your own and others' competence can be thrilling and empowering. Through working together to highlight strengths and address weaknesses, you empower yourself and others to go beyond expectations in discovering your collective potential. Trust of Capability grows when your co-workers get better at what they do, take more joy in doing it, and encourage others to follow their lead toward a more effective, vibrant workplace.

> *Developing your own and others' competence*
> *can be thrilling and empowering.*

Dealing with Disappointment

What about the times when your support of others' competence doesn't work out? When you trust your co-worker with a major project and he or she drops the ball?

> *Larry, a partner in an accounting firm, shared a hard lesson he learned: "Having Trust of Capability is not blind trust— you've got to follow your intuition. I allowed Susan, who was outwardly very confident, to 'snow' me. Susan's confidence overshadowed a slipshod approach to her books. I trusted her, but I should have followed my instincts. She didn't perform up to my expectations." By the time Larry realized Susan wasn't performing up to par, it was almost too late. The books were due, and Larry's co-worker had failed to deliver. Larry reflects: "The lesson for me is 'Do not be afraid to confront.' A lot of external distractions clouded my intuition. Because of my trust in this person, I made an assumption that Susan should know how to do this closing. I mistook her assertiveness and confidence for competence. I needed to trust my intuition."*

This story illustrates the hard lesson that trusting in others doesn't mean you should neglect your common sense. It's important to review each situation carefully "with open eyes" to determine whom you can trust with what. You may trust in a person's competence more than he or she does: this is a situation ripe for your coaching. Other times, you may feel like you should trust, but something is telling you otherwise: this is a situation that warrants more measured, controlled delegation of a major project. You need to listen to yourself and follow your intuition.

And there are times when, despite your co-worker's very best efforts, you may still be disappointed in results: "I asked you to do X; you gave it your best effort but came up short. I am disappointed." When a person has honestly tried to accomplish a task but failed due to lack of skill or aptitude, you may feel let down. It's important, however, to realize your colleague's behavior isn't a betrayal per se—it may be an honest shortfall in meeting your expectations. He may have not have been aware of his own shortcomings.

In these situations, it's vital that you take a close look at your role in the breakdown.

Did you provide him any support throughout the project? Did you hold back your trust, making it difficult for him to ask for help when he needed it? Did you not trust your intuition?

Contributing to the growth of others starts with raising your awareness of how you bring yourself to your relationships. Through reflecting on these questions, you may find you need to shift your perspective and be open to trusting yourself and others more fully. You may need to reframe habits, thoughts, and perceptions that have caused you to hold yourself and others back in the past. You can choose to behave differently in a way that better serves you and your relationships. Remember: trust begins with you.

Disappointments can be opportunities to reframe your behaviors and improve your relationships.

There will be times when you're disappointed, even frustrated, by a co-worker's performance—or lack thereof—but you'll benefit in the long run if you continue to provide support. You can help the person see how he or she can enter into similar situations differently in the future or illustrate how to tap into others and leverage their skills and support to be successful. An old Chinese proverb is as true today as ever: "If you want one year of prosperity, grow grain. If you want ten years of prosperity, grow trees. If you want one hundred years of prosperity, grow people."

Trust Building in Action
Reflecting on Your Experience

1. Where in your personal and work life do you experience high levels of trust in your capability?
2. Of the four behaviors that contribute to Trust of Capability, choose one or two that you feel represent opportunities for you to build more trust in your relationships with others.
   - Acknowledge people's skills and abilities
   - Allow people to make decisions
   - Involve others and seek their input
   - Help people learn skills

Trust Tip ▶ *When you trust others' capabilities, you demonstrate that you value their skills and abilities by giving them the latitude and flexibility to do their jobs, instead of micromanaging them. Doing so increases their commitment, motivation, and performance.*

Summary of The Three Cs of Trust

This chapter concludes our exploration of the Three Dimensions of Trust: The Three Cs. Before moving on to the next chapter where you will explore your readiness and willingness to trust, pause and review The Three Cs and their related behaviors in concert with one another.

Three Dimensions of Trust

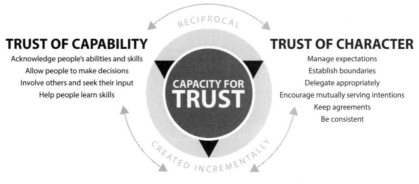

TRUST OF CAPABILITY

Acknowledge people's abilities and skills
Allow people to make decisions
Involve others and seek their input
Help people learn skills

TRUST OF CHARACTER

Manage expectations
Establish boundaries
Delegate appropriately
Encourage mutually serving intentions
Keep agreements
Be consistent

RECIPROCAL

CAPACITY FOR
TRUST

CREATED INCREMENTALLY

TRUST OF COMMUNICATION

Share information
Tell the truth
Admit mistakes
Give and receive constructive feedback
Maintain confidentiality
Speak with good purpose

In our work with people around the world, we're often asked if trustworthy relationships can thrive based on only one dimension of trust. The answer is: *No, not for long.* The Three Dimensions of Trust are interrelated. Although you may choose to focus on strengthening one dimension of trust within a specific relationship at a specific moment, your overall approach to building sustainably trustworthy connections must holistically incorporate all three dimensions and their respective behaviors.

To help clarify this truth, consider the last time you were hired for a position based on others' trust in your capability. Although your subject matter skills and talents landed you the job, you needed more than technical prowess to be effective in your team. Your boss, colleagues, direct reports, clients, and other stakeholders needed to know they could trust your word and character as deeply as they could trust your ability to complete a series of tasks. The Three Cs of Trust work hand in hand in the creation of sustainably trustworthy relationships, teams, and organizations. You have the opportunity to contribute to this trust-based community by practicing the behaviors within each dimension of trust. Trust begins with you.

CHAPTER FIVE

Your Readiness and Willingness to Trust

When our son Patrick turned thirteen, Dennis took him on a two-week "rite of passage" survival trek into the backcountry of the High Sierra of Yosemite National Park. The altitude was high, the air was thin, and the trail was dusty and difficult. This was heart of bear country, and on the fifth night, while Patrick and Dennis were cooking a pot of stew on the camp stove, a mother bear and three cubs strolled into their campsite. Within two minutes, the mother bear had scrambled up the tree just outside of camp where the food cache hung, taken one swipe at the nylon bag, and ripped the bottom open, dumping all of their provisions on the ground. For the next several hours, the mother bear taught her young cubs how to open freeze-dried food packages and granola energy bars. There was not much the backpackers could do but watch. These bears could outrun, out-climb, and out-swim the both of them. Because the animals were content eating their food, Dennis and Patrick turned in for the night inside their mountain tent.

The next morning, they surveyed the damage.

"What are we going to do now, Dad?" Patrick asked.

"*Trust and pray,*" Dennis replied.

"*No, really, Dad. What are we going to do? We are days from nowhere in the middle of the wilderness and our food is gone!*"

"*All we can do is trust and pray,*" Dennis repeated. As father and son picked up the torn food wrappers and empty containers scattered under the tree, a man appeared on the trail. This was significant because they hadn't seen anyone for the last two days.

"*Que pasa! What happened here?*" asked Miguel. Dennis described the previous night's visit from the bears. "*This is your lucky day. My buddy Juan and I have to cut our trek short and head back to the city today.*" An hour later, Miguel returned with a full sack of foodstuffs from their campsite over the ridge and handed it to Patrick.

"*Wow! This is exactly what I prayed for,*" Patrick exclaimed as he pulled out cans of Chef Boyardee Spaghetti O's, Swiss Miss Hot Chocolate packs, and Werther's Butterscotch candies. "*This trust and pray stuff really works!*"

The lesson of this story? Your willingness and readiness to trust yourself and others, particularly during times of ambiguity, is fundamental to how you show up and experience situations and how you experience others showing up in your life and at work.

How Your Capacity for Trust Developed

Building a trust-based workplace begins with you and how you bring yourself to your relationships. You want to work with people you trust and receive their trust in return. A step in attaining that goal is to understand how you interact with people. How

Capacity for Trust

READINESS AND WILLINGNESS TO TRUST SELF AND OTHERS

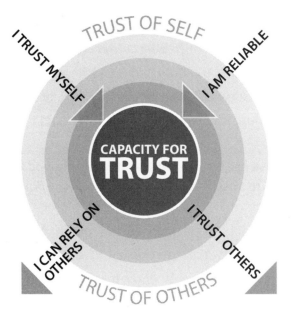

• Influences our beliefs and perceptions   • Updated by our experiences (positive and negative)

willing are you to trust others? How willing are you to trust yourself?

Your readiness and willingness to trust reflects your Capacity for Trust in yourself and those around you. When you trust yourself, you see yourself as reliable, dependable, and well intentioned. When you trust others, you have confidence in their judgment and intentions.

This developmental predisposition to trust began to form in the very early stages of your life and evolved throughout your childhood. The first two years of your youth were especially critical to this development. The level of stability, predictability, and attentiveness you received from your caregivers and other close connections during this time provided signals about who, how, and when to trust based on your positive and negative experiences.

Some people had early life experiences rich with support, comfort, safety, and nurturing. They found themselves surrounded by people they could rely on. Others may have had early life circumstances with inconsistent care, lack of safety, little nurturing, or without adults upon whom they could depend.

You've been influenced about who, how, and when to trust from the moment you were born.

Understandably, if you learned that others could be counted on to be there for you, your Capacity for Trust expanded, and you developed a readiness to enter into relationships by extending your trust until it was proven unsafe to do so. Conversely, if your upbringing was riddled with inconsistencies, letdowns, or upheavals, your Capacity for Trust contracted. You may have learned that it wasn't safe to trust. In this case, you may have developed a need for tangible evidence before you could be confident that others could be trusted.

Most people's childhoods were mixtures of calm and chaos, situations that caused trust to grow and contract accordingly. In these cases, it wasn't necessarily the ambiguity itself that influenced your Capacity for Trust but the skill with which your caregivers managed it.

Michelle's father served as a military intelligence officer, and throughout her childhood, her family moved every two years in response to his assignments. Michelle was born in Eritrea during Ethiopian rule, and as a young child, her first swim was in the Red Sea. Michelle's mother beamed when the emperor, Haile Selassie, held her infant daughter in his arms. The family later lived in Japan during the Vietnam War. After each new assignment, Michelle would kiss her father good-bye and never knew where he was going or when or if she would see him again. Before she was born, her father had been held in captivity during the Korean War. Michelle had heard the stories of his imprisonment, and she carried with her the knowledge that bad things happened to good people during wartime. Despite the family's constant relocation and changing, unpredictable environments, however, Michelle's mother and father created a level of consistency and continuity within their household. This stability expanded Michelle's Capacity for Trust—even in the midst of unimaginable change and heart-wrenching uncertainty.

Over time, as you developed mentally, emotionally, physically, and spiritually, you became more self-reliant and learned to trust your own perceptions and judgment. As you mastered developmental tasks that were appropriately acknowledged by your caregivers, you began to have confidence in your abilities. These early experiences influenced your willingness to take risks and to trust in your competence to resolve problems and overcome difficult situations.

Eventually, this approach evolved into a more complex understanding of the world. What began as an *I trust it because I can see it* attitude expanded to include the idea of reciprocity: *If I do something for you, will you do something for me?* As your thoughts grew in sophistication, you caught glimpses of the pinnacle of trusting relationships: *You have my word that you can depend on me, no matter what.*

As you progressed through young adulthood, your earliest conditioning still formed the basis of your knee-jerk reactions to situations; your *actual response*, however, may have matured. For example, when your friend didn't call like he said he would on a Saturday morning, your initial fear may have been that he found something better to do than play a pick-up basketball game with you. Even though you were hurt and angry, you decided to stay home and shoot hoops by yourself in your driveway instead of going to his house to confront him. Later that day, you learned that your friend had simply overslept and that he was sorry to have missed the opportunity to spend some time on the court. In this situation, your Capacity for Trust was tested. By giving the scenario time to play out, however, you learned that your fears were unfounded, and you were happy that you didn't jeopardize a friendship with a rash response.

Although your knee-jerk reactions to tested trust may remain, your actual responses can mature over time.

Your Capacity for Trust in both yourself and others continued to develop as you passed out of your teens and twenties and into full-fledged adulthood. As you matured, new relationships, personal development opportunities, and increasing professional pressures shaped your ability to have confidence in your surroundings and in your own approach to life. Over time, the lessons in trust (or distrust) from your earliest years were either strengthened or dismantled—often without your conscious awareness.

This lifetime of experiences influenced your readiness and willingness to trust today, your Capacity for Trust. This capacity influences your perceptions and beliefs. Your perceptions and beliefs influence your behavior. And your behavior is what builds or breaks trust. Trust begins with you.

Trust of Self

Trust in yourself is core to your sense of who you are. When you have a high level of trust in yourself, you feel centered and confident. You consider yourself dependable, reliable, and capable of fulfilling the expectations others have of you. This level of self-trust affects your workplace relationships. Those who have a healthy level of self-confidence tend to be trusted and relied upon more by others than those who have low self-trust.

Do you know that inner voice that asks you questions about your capabilities? *Can I do this? Am I right for this job? Am I able to live up to the new expectations of me? Can I be relied on to keep up with the changes around here? Will I say and do the right things in my relationships? Are my strengths strong enough to compensate for my weaknesses?*

Each of us has asked these questions of ourselves at one time or another during our working lives—particularly during change or when the stakes are high and there are unknowns. When you have an innate trust of self, you're more inclined to answer yes to these lingering questions. You find a starting point within yourself from which you can move forward. You know that you're able to draw on your relationships with others and that you are worthy of support. When you answer no to these questions, you may find yourself paralyzed by fear, wallowing in confusion, self-doubt, and a reluctance to rely on others or ask them for help.

Trusting yourself gives you a starting point to face challenges.

The trust you have in yourself is your starting point in your approach to relationships and life—as well as the foundation for your self-esteem and sense of identity. Self-trust is the glue that holds you together in times of trouble and the inspiration that spurs you to unimaginable achievement. With it, you're positioned to become the best possible version of yourself. Without it, you're stuck in stasis, repeating patterns, reliving worn-out scenarios, and missing golden opportunities to take your personal and professional relationships to the next level.

Your Capacity for Trust directly affects your attitude toward taking risks and trying new things. You are capable of accomplishing only what you believe is possible. For example, if a pole-vaulter doesn't believe she's capable of clearing eighteen feet, the chances are pretty slim she will. If you're given a task and you assume there's no way to complete it, you'll probably prove yourself right. If, however, you realistically assess the situation, trust in yourself, trust others to lend a hand when needed, and strive to meet the goal, you *will* be successful.

An expanded Capacity for Trust enables you to deal with uncertainty, navigate ambiguity, and take calculated chances because you know you can rely on yourself and others to overcome challenges.

Sandy received a promotion offer for a high-profile position in charge of the central operations center of a large telecommunications company. Although she had never seen herself in such a managerial role, she could see how the assignment would serve as a stepping-stone to reach her professional aspirations. Sandy considered the position with quiet excitement, coupled with strong anxiety and fear. Could she trust herself to do the job? Did she have the necessary technical skills? She came close to turning down the position.

Sandy shared her concerns with others, who helped her see how her current skills laid the foundation for this new role. The conversations about her competencies helped quiet her fears, and she began to identify the people around her she could rely on to further develop her technical knowledge. Sandy accepted the job and trusted in herself and her colleagues to develop and execute a sound strategy. She succeeded in her new position and earned another promotion two years later.

When your Capacity for Trust in yourself is contracted, you're inclined to sell yourself short, shying away from reasonable risks and new opportunities. Doubting your skills, you become paralyzed by fear, confusion, and doubt and fall victim to the little voice that questions your capabilities. You struggle to find a starting point, are less willing to ask others for help, and overestimate the gravity of obstacles in your path. Interestingly, you also risk falling into perfectionistic patterns as you strive to battle your doubts with irrefutable evidence of your own skill and talent. The signs of contracted Capacity for Trust are often subtle or so ingrained in your natural habits they can be difficult for you to see and even harder to fight back against.

In Chapter 10, we'll be sharing four pathways to help you expand your Capacity for Trust in yourself. These pathways will serve as resources to ground you in your relationship with *you* and empower you to develop a strong sense of trust in your own perceptions and abilities. With this heightened level of self-trust, you'll be better positioned to extend your trust to others.

How to Talk Back to the Voice of Doubt in Your Head

- Identify past successes that paved the way to your current position.
- Think about the challenges you faced along the way to those successes.
- List the specific skills and talents that allowed you to overcome past challenges.
- Think about the resources you tapped into to learn about and get better at the things you needed to succeed.
- Think about the help you received from others as you stretched and grew.
- Explore how your past creativity, strength, and support network could be leveraged to help you overcome your current self-doubts.

Trust of Others

When you trust others, you view them as dependable and reliable in fulfilling your expectations. Do you hear your inner voice ask: *Can I really trust my co-workers? Will they tell me the truth when it counts? Are they able to do what it takes when the chips are down? Can I trust them to do their part?*

Your Capacity for Trust in others is critical to your workplace relationships. When you have an expanded ability to trust in others, you're able to work in a fluid fashion. You extend your trust until you have clear evidence that you shouldn't. You share information, tell the truth, and leverage your own and others' skills. You relax in your need to control others' contributions to your shared work.

When you have an expanded Capacity for Trust, you extend trust to others until you have evidence that you shouldn't.

Your Capacity for Trust affects how you work with your co-workers, boss, customers, and suppliers. Healthy relationships are based on trust, not legal contracts or money-back guarantees. Trust requires reciprocity. Generally speaking, the more you give, the more you get. Mutually trusting relationships grow the more you operate from mutually serving intentions, keep agreements, and respect other people's abilities.

When you have an expanded Capacity for Trust, you're more inclined to give others the benefit of the doubt when they let you down. You suspend judgment or criticism and make the effort to discover the reasons behind letdowns. For instance, when someone doesn't come through for you, your inner voice is less inclined to turn to angry thoughts. *I should have known I couldn't trust her* becomes *She's usually very reliable. What might have happened to have caused her not to deliver on her promise? Maybe she was sick or had a family emergency!* When you trust others, you remain open to the natural path of life, continuing to trust until it's clear it's no longer appropriate to do so. You approach each person with sincere interest and concern rather than with suspicion and readiness to lay blame.

When you have a contracted Capacity for Trust in others, you experience your workplace very differently. You're more likely to judge, criticize, and jump to conclusions. You may tend to withhold information, keep your ideas and concerns close to your chest, and not rely on others or ask for help when you need it. You may refrain from delegating even minor tasks with the belief that no one can do it as well as you. Communication breaks down; effectiveness and efficiency suffer. The stress, doubt, and fear that come with contracted Capacity for Trust take a toll on your health and home life. The ability to trust others is more than just a theoretical nicety—it's a vital component to your success on the job and to your enjoyment of satisfying relationships.

You're more inclined to give others the benefit of the doubt when you have an expanded Capacity for Trust.

Generally speaking, the more trust you give, the more you get. Although there are no guarantees in any relationship—personal or professional—it's easier to trust others when you trust yourself. Your Capacity for Trust anchors you through the turbulence of disappointments and frustrations in one relationship and allows you to reap the benefits of many trusting and satisfying relationships in the course of your personal and professional life. When you expand your capacity, you increase your trustworthiness. When others receive your trust, they are more likely to give their trust. Trust begets trust. And trust begins with you.

The more trust you give, the more trust you get.

The Starting Point for Your Relationships (Trust Begins with You)

You trust others in proportion to how much you trust yourself. Right now, you may be thinking *Wait a minute. There are plenty of times when I trust myself more than I trust other people, and rightfully so!* That may be true. But let's unpack that thought, using what you've already learned about your unique Capacity for Trust. When you withhold your trust, it's often because a specific previous experience (or set of experiences) taught you it wasn't safe to rely on or trust that person or situation. When something isn't "safe," it means there is a chance it could hurt you—physically or emotionally, personally or professionally.

We all get let down (and let others down). Betrayal is a natural part of relationships. Yet, some of those hurts are easier to recover from than others. Why is that? The answer lies in your confidence in your *ability* to recover. When you don't have this confidence—this capacity to rely on and trust yourself to recover from whatever hurt you may suffer—then you're far more likely to withhold your trust from others.

Conversely, when you carry within yourself a strong attitude that even if things don't go well, you can deal with the outcomes, learn from them, and get even stronger, then you're more likely to take the risk of putting your trust in others. You can see the potential of collaboration, delegation, and partnership, and understand that you can achieve far more with others than you ever could on your own—even if that "letting go and trusting" process isn't always a smooth one. At the end of the day, self-trust enables you to trust others, even when there is a chance that your trust may not be returned or rewarded.

At this point, it may seem like we're espousing that you should always trust yourself and others to the highest degree possible. That couldn't be further from the truth. Some people and situations shouldn't be trusted. And there are times that it doesn't make sense to trust yourself—such as when your knowledge or experience is lacking, your energy levels are low, or the realities of

---

How to Build Confidence that You Can Handle Broken Trust

- Imagine the worst possible outcome of a theoretical hurt or disappointment.
- You resist talking with people who remind you of someone else with whom you had a bad experience.
- Open yourself to how you'd feel if your trust was broken in this way.
- Don't run from your feelings. Sit with them and explore them.
- Think about how you would move forward from this period of hurt. What actions would you take? Who would you reach to for help?
- Walk yourself through your "recovery" process and visualize your arrival on the other side of your letdown, healthy and whole.
- Finally, consider how likely your "worst outcome" really is. Develop a list of more realistic outcomes from placing your trust in others.
- Practice trusting yourself by stepping outside your comfort zone. Extend trust to a colleague in a way you normally wouldn't. Repeat this exercise and watch your confidence grow in dealing with the outcomes, both large and small.

---

time or geography prevent you from achieving your goals effectively. We're not talking about blind trust, but *appropriate* trust.

It is not always appropriate to trust; some people and situations shouldn't be trusted.

Never let go of your instincts when approaching relationships with others. Just be aware of what you're bringing with you to each interaction. Remember, your *Capacity for Trust* isn't the key: your *awareness of your Capacity for Trust* is—awareness—and the choices you make through that awareness. The intention is for you to identify your assumptions and predispositions toward trusting others in order to manage knee-jerk reactions that hold you back from developing appropriate, healthy, working relationships.

There is a difference between not trusting someone because it's not appropriate and not trusting someone because you don't trust *yourself* to handle the fallout if things go awry. This lack of trust is usually based on your previous experiences and your projection of those experiences onto a current situation. All human relationships have the potential of going awry—that's a job hazard of being human, living consciously, and trying to make meaningful connections with others. The aim is to accept the fragility of trusting relationships and move through it in order to develop appropriate trust in yourself and others.

Trust Building in Action

Reflecting on Your Experience

1. Think about your relationships with others in your personal life. How do you bring yourself to those relationships? Do you tend to assume that others should be trusted, or do you wait for people to prove they are trustworthy? Whichever your tendency, how does it affect the quality of your personal relationships?

2. Think about your professional relationships. How do you bring yourself to those interactions? Do you trust until you receive evidence you shouldn't? Or do you withhold your trust until you feel assured that others deserve your confidence? How does your approach affect the effectiveness of your workplace relationships?

Trust Tip ▶ *Your Capacity for Trust influences your perceptions and beliefs, your perceptions and beliefs influence your behavior, and your behavior builds or breaks trust in your relationships.*

CHAPTER SIX

How You Trust

When our son, Will, was a little boy we put him on cross-country skis. At the foot of his first big hill his voice quivered, "I don't think I can do it, Daddy." Dennis gave his son's shoulder a quick squeeze. "Sure you can, Will. I'm right here with you. We'll take it one step at a time." On the way up the long, steep hill, Will experienced some moments of struggle, fear, and anxiety. Once the pair had finally reached the top, Dennis leaned down and encouraged our son, "Turn around and look, Will, and see what you did." When Will turned around, he couldn't believe what he saw. He had climbed all the way up this long, steep hill by himself. His trust and confidence soared. He shouted out to the heavens, "Let's do it again, Daddy. Let's do it again!" And again and again they did.

The Four Questions of Your Capacity for Trust

Like Will, before you tackle a big new challenge, you may have trepidations and question your capability. As you become aware of your current Capacity for Trust, you realize just how deeply it affects your perceptions, beliefs, and behaviors—and the level of unease you feel when facing new or uncomfortable situations. The material you're getting ready to dive into next will expand on this awareness. By reflecting on a series of four questions, you're going to learn more about yourself and what you need to do to expand your Capacity for Trust—both in yourself and in others.

Trust building does not require you to *change* who you are, but rather to be *aware* of who you are. You need to be honest about what you need from relationships, about what you have to give, and about what behaviors within The Three Cs you must practice to earn your own and others' trust. By raising your self-awareness, you put yourself in the strongest position to make the best choices about how to behave, even in low-trust situations. The following four questions will help you make those choices and understand why others' behaviors differ from your own.

Increasing your self-awareness allows you to make the best choices about how to behave in challenging situations.

A final note before moving into the questions: your answers may depend on the various situations in which you find yourself. There are no "wrong" answers. Each question should be viewed as a sliding scale with the understanding that context influences how you respond. We ask these questions to open your awareness to different ways of thinking and behaving—and to understand how those approaches influence your ability to trust yourself and others. The goal of working through these questions is for you to be able to meet your co-workers where they are and work together to get to where you all want to be—a trusting, compassionate, and productive workplace.

Let's get started.

How You Trust

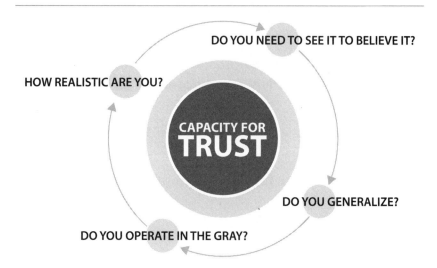

How Realistic Are You?

Do you place a reasonable amount of trust in yourself or others to meet specific goals and deadlines? Or do you routinely underestimate what's needed to get the job done, placing yourself and others in uncomfortable positions at the eleventh hour of a promised deliverable? When you are realistic, you more accurately judge the time, skill level, and resources required to complete a project.

The degree to which your projections are tied to concrete, attainable outcomes indicates how realistic you are, which in turn influences how you take risks. Those who tend toward a high degree of realism may take calculated chances and develop trust in incremental steps. They're more apt to assess the risks involved before placing confidence in others. They check assumptions and reevaluate the judgments they form about people and situations. They break large projects down into manageable pieces, encourage others to collaborate in order to meet goals, and give people the time and space they need to do their jobs.

The more realistic you are, the better you're able to judge what's actually needed to get the job done.

Those with contracted degrees of realism often take unreasonable risks, believing it's possible to overcome insurmountable challenges at all costs. They trust themselves more than others to take on important tasks, even if they don't personally possess the necessary skills or expertise to complete the work. They often fail to provide necessary information to teammates or reach out for help when needed, jeopardizing the company's reputation and relationships with clients.

At first blush, it may seem that being unrealistic is wholly without merit. That's not entirely true. Some of the greatest achievements of mankind have occurred because people have forged ahead in order to achieve "the impossible," despite all available evidence that the risk of failure was nearly absolute. It's important to remember that each person's view of "the impossible" is different. Writing a book while working full time and raising a family may be viewed by some as unrealistic. To others, it appears more like a series of manageable hurdles to clear on the way to inevitable success. Climbing Mount Everest without supplemental oxygen was considered a suicide mission—until Messner and Habeler accomplished the feat in 1978.

Remember, the lesson in discovering your predisposition to being realistic is to make you aware of your natural tendencies, so that you can be honest with yourself and others about the risks you're taking. Being unrealistic can be the launching point for

> ## How to Spot When You're Being Unproductively Unrealistic
>
> - You find yourself running from meeting to meeting or call to call with little time to get actual work completed. As a result you work late nights and weekends to get caught up.
> - You find that your product or projects are being pushed out the door before they meet your organization's standards of quality.
> - You aren't able to name your top three priorities, but instead rattle off more than a dozen "vital" initiatives or goals.
> - When you review your day, you realize you spent more time dictating (or coercing) than listening.
> - You notice others have stopped reaching out to you to give or receive help or support.

big things, but the people involved need to be aware of what "it" will take and what's on the line if they're not successful. When equipped with this knowledge, both you and others can make informed decisions to "buy in" (or not) to your ideas, timelines, or deliverables. If failure does occur, a baseline of trust can be maintained—if there's a willingness to learn from the experience.

Do You Need to See It to Believe It?

Are you able to take direction according to philosophy, values, and intuition? Or do you need concrete facts, figures, and hard evidence in order to trust your marching orders? Do you take a "prove it first" approach to working with others? Or are you able to take their words at face value?

The degree to which you need to "see it to believe it" influences your ability to let go, delegate, trust in the promises of others, and not feel the need to be in control. People who don't need concrete, tangible evidence to move forward are usually more willing to give others the benefit of the doubt, deal with ambiguity and uncertainty, and approach relationships with greater flexibility and freedom.

Letting go of your need to "see it to believe it" allows you to trust in others' approach to work—and life.

Of course, different jobs demand different approaches. People in senior leadership positions are generally more comfortable creating tasks and action items according to "the ideal" of theoretical mission statements. They sorely need "boots on the ground" to give them accurate, honest feedback about their strategic decisions— feedback that's grounded in tangible, concrete realities on the front lines. Neither group is wrong in its predisposition toward abstract or concrete thinking in a given circumstance—so long as they recognize the value the other viewpoint brings to the table.

We're not espousing that you should always strive toward a "what might be" approach or settle comfortably into a "what is" frame of mind. The point of this question is for you to identify the camp from which you usually operate, understand why you operate that way, and then begin to think about the specific people or situations in your life that push you out of your comfort zone. Do you trust them less than you would if they approached life and work the way you did? Can you take the first steps toward recognizing the value of their positions? Being open to others who approach things differently than you builds trusting relationships. We all want to be seen and valued for who we are and what we bring to the table.

How to Spot When You May Be Missing the Value of Others' Approach to Work

- Your gut tells you that people are telling you what they think you want to hear rather than what is really on their mind.

- You feel your blood pressure go through the roof when colleagues challenge your position or approach.

- You find yourself cut out of high-level discussions because you've become known as a naysayer.

- You notice people come to you for reports only on things that have already happened and never to ask you for new ideas about how to make your workplace better in the future.

- You find yourself surrounded by people who never ask you for something you have to stretch to deliver.

Do You Operate in the Gray?

Are you inclined to base your decisions on black-and-white, right-or-wrong, and good-or-bad criteria? Are you prone to writing people off when they make a mistake? How comfortable are you with ambiguity? Do you find stimulation in taking in the multifaceted aspects of a situation or relationship?

The extent to which you're able to operate "in the gray" and consider extenuating circumstances affects your ability to make sophisticated, informed decisions about people, situations, and ideas. When you're comfortable with ambiguity, you're able to see multiple ways to approach a given scenario, each with its own pros and cons. You're able to appreciate that each person has strengths and weaknesses and that their needs may vary based upon the situation. You're more inclined to give the benefit of the doubt, ask questions, and test your assumptions. You can engage with others—and with life—with a healthy mix of positive expectation and skepticism.

When you aren't comfortable in the gray zone, you tend to see the world in more simplistic terms—a "right" way and a "wrong" way. People are either "all good" or "all bad." This approach generally leads to you being seen as strong-willed, rigid, and unwilling to compromise. This can be highly problematic in the workplace as you try to juggle the inherent complexities of unique personalities, unexplored opportunities, and deep-rooted system problems. If you're constantly making snap judgments and simplistic arguments, you set yourself up to be left out in the cold when it comes to getting the marquis assignments or coveted promotions. Moreover, you miss the opportunity to build valuable relationships with people who, although not perfect, are able to contribute to your learning and quality of life.

When you aren't comfortable with ambiguity, you may see the world in more simplistic terms: black-and-white or good-and-bad.

Does all of this mean that it's *always* best to operate in the gray? No. There are times when a cut-and-dry approach is imperative. Consider the result if an EMT ruminated on perfect technique before jumping in to give CPR. Or if a mother googled the latest treatise on traffic-flow patterns before running into a busy intersection to save her runaway child. The same is true for the workplace. We've all been in meetings where "analysis paralysis" is holding up forward movement. Sometimes, a decision just needs to be made, even if the best choice is not unequivocally clear.

There is a time and place for in-depth analysis, just as there is for rapid action; the key is to know the difference between the

---

How to Spot When You Need to Rethink Your Black-and-White Approach

---

- You routinely discover your snap decisions weren't the right ones for the good of your team or organization.

- Your circle of professional and personal friends has narrowed to only those who agree with you.

- You find yourself reluctant to reconstruct a "burned bridge" so you avoid tapping an alienated colleague's expertise on a new project.

- Your boss, colleagues, and employees have stopped bringing you new ideas or suggestions for changes.

- You find yourself thinking about where you "would have been" in your career (or personal life) if you'd just been able to relax your need for control.

---

two. Once you can spot how you and others naturally approach situations—and compare those behaviors with appropriate actions—*then* you can begin to adjust your behaviors to be more productive and responsive to your co-workers' needs. This awareness will help you build confidence in your own capabilities and develop trusting relationships with other people as they learn that you value their starting points.

Do You Generalize?

Do you assume that whatever is true for you is true for others? When you have a good or bad experience with one member of a group, do you automatically generate good or bad feelings about the rest of its members? Or do take the approach that others may not always align with your approach to life and work? Are you comfortable taking each person on his or her own terms regardless of group affiliation or context?

When you project your own values and beliefs onto others and stigmatize crowds of people based on one interaction, you risk your ability to make sound decisions and to build trust. Recognizing your limitations or strengths in this area of your life can help you remove stresses in your relationships and develop a healthier approach to your work. When you're able to meet people where they are (instead of where you imagine or want them to be), you open up possibilities for meaningful, enduring connections and informed decision making. Additionally, you ease up in your assessments of your own and others' performance, and take in the reality that failure isn't necessarily indicative of poor character or "bad" organizations, but rather a natural occurrence in the course of human development.

Meeting people where they are—instead of where you imagine them to be—opens up possibilities for deeper connections.

When people are different from you, you may find it difficult to trust them—especially if you've had past negative experiences with people "like them." For example, if you've previously struggled to collaborate with a key staffer over in accounting, then you may be hesitant to trust anyone else from that department—regardless of their attitude, aptitude, or approach to your shared work. This is understandable and a natural human response. We've all been conditioned to attach labels to negative experiences. Doing so, however, is a disservice to ourselves and to others as we try to build trusting relationships.

How to Spot When You're Limiting Yourself by Overgeneralizing about Others

- You resist talking with people who seem different from you.
- You resist talking with people who remind you of someone else with which you had a bad experience.
- You can't remember the last time you welcomed someone into your life who forced you to stretch and grow.
- You're routinely mystified—and frustrated—by others' approach to life and work.
- You find yourself justifying your opinions about certain groups of people with out-of-date information or vague perceptions about what they think or how they behave.
- You're genuinely surprised when you enjoy a conversation with one of "those people."

Again, the goal in assessing your approach to making generalizations is to make you aware of how you approach your relationships. There is a time and a place for generalizing situations and people. Remember, we're not espousing blind trust, but appropriate trust. This trust is stymied—and broken—by making rash assumptions and refusing to own your initial overgeneralizations. This trust is built by seeking to understand, refining expectations, and behaving accordingly.

Your Capacity for Trust Changes over Time

Your Capacity for Trust is dynamic. It expands and contracts based on your experiences and the situations in which you find yourself. You have the ability to expand your Capacity for Trust by applying the four questions just discussed to your relationships. You can choose to evolve in your understanding of the bigger picture of who, why, when, and how much people trust. And you can use this understanding to crack the code of your struggles to connect with others and with yourself. Trust is built through self-awareness and adjusting your practice of The Three Cs behaviors accordingly. Trust begins with you.

Your Capacity for Trust expands and contracts based on your experiences and the situations in which you find yourself.

Trust Building in Action

Reflecting on Your Experience

In order to understand how each of the four questions influences your Capacity for Trust, think about the following questions:

1. Why are some people willing to take risks? How willing are you to take risks?

2. Why are some people willing to accept the promises of others? How willing are you to take others' words at face value?

3. Why are some people willing to make a snap judgment based on one interaction? Do you find yourself jumping to conclusions?

4. Why are some people comfortable with people whose thinking is radically different from their own? How comfortable are you with people who force you to stretch and question your assumptions?

Trust Tip ▶ *The more self-aware you are, the less you'll be affected by your knee-jerk responses to trusting situations and people, and the more you'll be able to make conscious choices about your behaviors.*

CHAPTER SEVEN

How Trust Is Broken: Betrayal

"I'm really upset with Lynette!" said Patrick, an outreach coordinator. "She didn't deliver her part of the project as she promised. She let me down and she let her other co-workers down. There is no longer trust on this team."

"I don't understand why John went to Craig to talk about the concern he has with me," Scott, an executive assistant, said. "Why didn't he come to me directly and give me a chance to address it with him? It hurt to hear about this from Craig. Now I wonder who else John talked to about me. Can I really trust him?"

"We trusted Donald, and he betrayed us!" Elena, a retail clerk, said angrily, referring to her boss. "He lied to us. I've got a hollow feeling in the pit of my stomach. I'm angry and hurt. I don't like working in an environment where I'm lied to and betrayed. I spend too much energy watching my back! I don't know who or what I can believe anymore."

Betrayal is a big word. You may view it as dark and negative; a connotation that triggers painful memories you'd rather forget. It may represent a significant occurrence of hurt and deceit in your life—perhaps a time when you were lied to, cheated on, or taken advantage of. But in reality, betrayal occurs with each and every instance of broken trust—regardless of its size. That is the simple truth. It's also true that every single one of us has been betrayed and has betrayed others, even if we haven't meant to. There is betrayal among colleagues, bosses, and employees—within families, neighborhoods, and churches. You and your friends betray one another, and we all at times betray ourselves. Betrayal is universal and a natural outcome of interacting with other people.

You may not be comfortable with this truth. You may want to run away from it and scramble toward the positive energy that comes from trustworthy relationships. Yet, to capture that energy, you must appreciate its absence. Betrayal and trust ebb and flow as inevitably as the tide in your relationships. You pour your heart into building trust and revel in its presence. Then, because you're human and can't sustain perfection, you slip up and betrayal pulls your trust out to sea. You work harder, and trust returns. You stumble, and it's diminished again. There is no conquering this natural cycle of trust and distrust. You can only embrace it, learn from it, and be ready to handle the next big wave.

Every single one of us has been
betrayed and has betrayed others.

So when you feel that you or others have broken trust in your workplace, it doesn't mean that you work with "bad" people, that you're naive, or that you yourself are of questionable morals. You're simply engaging with the human experience as best as you're able. Trust will be built. Trust will be broken. By you, and by all of us. The more holistic and realistic your view of trust in your relationships, the better you'll understand why betrayals occur and how you can show up differently the next time by practicing the behaviors of The Three Cs more faithfully.

This understanding of betrayal will help you to trust again when you've been betrayed, take ownership when you've betrayed another, and have empathy for the people in your life when they speak to you about their pain. Your wisdom will transform you into a guiding light both at work and at home, illuminating the path toward wholeness and health for everyone around you. Trust begins with you.

Let's continue by learning more about the shades of betrayal and their impact.

The Betrayal Continuum

Betrayal takes different shapes and forms and comes in a variety of sizes. It occurs on a continuum from unintentional to intentional and from minor to major. Intentional betrayal is a self-serving action committed with the purpose of hurting, damaging, or harming another person. Unintentional betrayal is self-serving

BETRAYAL

BREACH OF TRUST OR A PERCEPTION OF A BREACH
- Minor to major
- Unintentional or intentional
- Energy depleting

THE BETRAYAL CONTINUUM

MINOR (EXAMPLES)		MAJOR (EXAMPLES)	
UNINTENTIONAL	**INTENTIONAL**	**UNINTENTIONAL**	**INTENTIONAL**
Repeatedly arriving late for work	Gossiping, backbiting	Restructuring resulting in layoffs	Disclosing proprietary information
Not keeping agreements	Accepting credit for another's work	Delegating without giving authority	Sabotaging data systems

but is committed without the conscious knowledge of how it will hurt others. Major behaviors grab your attention right away, whereas minor betrayals are more able to be ignored—at least in the short-term.

Major Betrayal

Major betrayals impact you immediately and dramatically at your deepest core. Major *intentional* betrayals are often the result of fear and self-serving interests and include situations in which people deliberately fail to honor their commitments, knowingly withhold information, deceive fellow co-workers, or even sabotage others' work to further their own ends. Major intentional betrayals are hurtful, ill-intended words or actions that break down trusting relationships. As one concerned employee told us, "It's especially painful when you're stabbed in the back without warning by those closest to you. It knocks you off your feet."

Major *unintentional* betrayal is often associated with the insensitivity with which change is managed related to reorganizations, shifts in strategy, mergers, acquisitions, lay-offs, and reassignments.

> *After working sixteen years in his dream job in enrollment services with a major university, Mike received a mass email that he was being let go due to restructuring. He discovered that the message had been sent to thirteen other people as well. "I had put my heart and soul into that job," he said. "And they didn't even have the decency to tell me I was fired to my face. It was completely unexpected." Even after he found another position with a competitor, Mike felt bitter and resentful toward his former employer. They had made him feel incidental, disposable, and worthless. "I wanted to*

get back at them, to show them they had made a bad mistake when they let me go."

Minor Betrayal

Although major betrayals do happen, most forms of betrayal are minor. Minor betrayals can be *intentional,* such as when people gossip behind one anothers' backs, spin the truth rather than own it, and hide their personal agendas. Or they can be *unintentional,* such as failing to pass along pertinent information, deliver on a promise, or tap others' expertise as a project progresses. It's important to remember that betrayals are considered unintentional, not because people don't intend to act in a certain way but because those actions aren't intended to cause harm to others.

Although minor betrayals can be small and subtle, the accumulation of their impact is not. Because they happen each and every day in the workplace, they have the potential to add up to pervasive, insidious drains on your self-confidence and energy.

Take a look at the box (on the next page) of minor betrayals people tell us they experience. Do you recognize any of these? Our research shows that 90 percent of employees experience these types of trust breaking behaviors frequently. Rather than deal directly with these transgressions, people let them go unaddressed. They are swept under the carpet or ignored. *Oh, let's not waste time on that little stuff. Let's get on with it. We have too much to do.*

Although you may try to deny, ignore, minimize, or rationalize these small breaches of trust, they don't go away. Unresolved, they grow and contribute to negative feelings in your relationships and workplace. Their cumulative weight is equivalent to, if not greater than, a major betrayal. They create an "energy leak" that leaves you feeling spent, discouraged, and unproductive. Your

Common Workplace Minor Betrayals

- Gossip
  - ▶ "Because there's little direct communication from people 'in the know,' everyone gossips and makes up what they think is really happening."
  - ▶ "I don't trust anyone around here. Everyone talks about everyone else behind their backs."
- Shoot the messenger
  - ▶ "I've been shot down over and over again, and I've started to believe that no one cares about the truth."
  - ▶ "When people bring up an issue, they get a response that goes something like, 'What concern is it of yours? Don't bother; it's none of your business.'"
- Accept credit for work performed by others
  - ▶ "Around here, people take credit for others' work or blame another department (to upper management) when things go badly."
  - ▶ "I've had to start hiding my ideas from my colleagues until I pitch them to the leadership team. I know my work will get stolen otherwise."
- Send mixed messages
  - ▶ "Some areas of my organization have leaders that say one thing and do another. Their constant contradictions have permanently eliminated the trust people used to have in them."
  - ▶ "People's actions don't always match the messages that are delivered around here."
- Refuse to consider new ideas or methods
  - ▶ "Some people on my team are unwilling to try a new approach, and they make it really hard for anyone who is."
  - ▶ "I could teach these supervisors a lot, but they think they know everything."
- Retribution and retaliation
  - ▶ "In our team meetings, there is a lot of backstabbing. It has become a very political place."
  - ▶ "When a mistake emerges out of a group effort, everyone looks for a single individual to blame instead of the group taking responsibility."

enthusiasm and interest are replaced with exhaustion and apathy. You and others move from feeling pride in your workplace to wondering *Why do I stay here?* You close your hearts and minds to one another, and even to yourselves, as you attempt to protect your core from the attacks of a painful work environment.

Your Experience of Betrayal

How you position your experience of a breach of trust along the betrayal continuum depends on your perception of intent and impact—in other words, the degree of a person's intention to harm you and the amount of pain, damage, or loss you experience. For instance, accepting credit for someone else's work may be a minor intentional betrayal in one circumstance, but if the person who falsely accepts credit gains greatly at the other's expense (for example, if he or she gets promoted for work a co-worker deserved credit for), it becomes a major intentional betrayal.

The opportunity for betrayal in any relationship at work or in your personal life is influenced by the amount or degree of trust you have in that individual, situation, team, or organization. An important aspect of trust has to do with expectations. If you have few or no expectations, you aren't as susceptible to disappointment, hurt, or strong feelings of betrayal. If, however, you have higher expectations and greater involvement and loyalty in the relationship, you are more vulnerable to betrayal. The more you have invested of yourself in a relationship, the more deeply hurt you may feel by a breach of trust.

It's not necessary that you diagnose your experience of betrayal to determine if it was major, minor, intentional, or unintentional. There is no right or wrong answer. We provide you with this framework of betrayal to help you understand your experiences and the vulnerability of trust. Whether a betrayal is major or minor, intentional or unintentional, the experience affects your Capacity for Trust in both yourself and others. Often, the impacts of major and accumulative minor betrayal are the same.

The Impact of Betrayal in the Workplace

Betrayals fray the fabric of relationships. Major betrayals cut the cords of connection between people; minor betrayals wear away at them bit by bit. Trust is energy producing; betrayal is energy depleting. Trust feeds performance; betrayal eats away at it.

Major betrayal clouds peoples' thinking, saps their motivation, and derails creativity. In a climate of major betrayal, productivity plummets. You don't need to read the news headlines to understand how the major betrayals of corporate scandals and ethical breaches cost companies, customers, employees, and stockholders billions of dollars.

Minor betrayals contribute incrementally to disengagement. Rather than being focused on doing their work, people spend time and energy protecting themselves. The office hallways, break rooms, and dining halls are filled with the whispers of people talking about occasions of breached trust and betrayal and wondering *How much longer can I cope? When will something be done? I thought I belonged here; now I'm not sure. Maybe I don't have what it takes after all.*

Minor betrayals are deceptive in impact. As they mount, they have the power to thoroughly dismantle an organization's morale, productivity, and overall effectiveness. They disrupt focus and concentration, and they create a cyclone of wasted energy within a rising tide of emotional upheaval. Betrayal is systemic; it affects the entire organization and everyone in it.

Charlotte, vice president of a Fortune 50 corporation, oversaw the implementation of the company's new performance management system. She overhauled her organization's approach and developed and rolled out a leadership development-training program, among a host of other initiatives. She executed her plans throughout the company, worldwide, in record time. Charlotte had a 150-person global unit of highly committed and very talented people with deep pride for the work they do. This unit facilitated initiatives throughout the company that regularly make tangible improvements in people's lives.

The unit paid a high price during three restructurings in two years, however, with the loss of 35 percent of its people and significant budget cuts across the board. Despite Charlotte's best efforts to keep her team aligned, little things began to fall through the cracks. Channels of communication and collaboration—already challenged to include people working all over the world—gradually broke down. Roles and responsibilities shifted, leaving decision-making boundaries blurred. Expectations began to go unfulfilled or unspoken.

Anxiety levels in the company began to rise. People no longer understood the direction of their unit or the direction of the company. They didn't know what the future held and didn't have a place to go to talk about it. This created mistrust and misunderstanding. People went at one another's throats: fighting for resources, hoarding information, and working at cross-purposes with one another. Quality of work declined, the timeline to delivery went drastically off course, and the group's reputation was compromised. High levels of trust had previously enabled Charlotte and her unit to succeed, but when trust diminished, the unit's overall perfor-mance declined.

Charlotte's organization suffered a series of minor betrayals that mounted as change was mismanaged. Everyone knows that change occurs. People no longer expect a stable organizational structure or environment. They realize that leaders cannot guar-antee tomorrow. But they do expect—and deserve—acknowl-edgement of and respect for the impact change has on their lives and relationships.

Trust feeds performance; betrayal eats away at it.

When reassignments, firings, or demotions are handled insensitively or without due attention and respect to their impact on people directly and indirectly, trust breaks down. People start wondering about the direction the organization is mov-ing, how they fit in, and if they want to fit in. They ponder *What is it going to be like to work here?* Or they worry whether they'll even have jobs at all. Rather than step up and take on new chal-lenges the organizational changes require, people are contracted and distracted. Rather than look forward, they look backward and become attached to "the way it used to be."

> *"We were downsized twice in one year. When people left, we lost relationships," Marlon, a draftsman in an architectural firm, shared with us. "Yet we've been expected to behave as if nothing happened, to simply focus on getting the job done. The loss of those relationships hurt, and it hurt even more that leadership did not recognize that. We needed to grieve."*

Whether it's rooted in organizational change or "business as usual" interactions between co-workers, betrayal hurts. It hurts because people have endured disappointment and suffered loss. They may have lost professional opportunities, close working relationships, or their hopes of what might have been for the future. When people hurt, they may want to get even. As trust begets trust, betrayal begets betrayal.

The Effect of Betrayal on Your Capacity for Trust

Betrayal has deep impact. It goes to the core of human vulnerability, cutting through to your deepest emotional layers to affect your Capacity for Trust in both yourself and others. As one employee sadly shared, "This betrayal makes me feel angry, sad, and lost. It destroys my faith in the betrayer, but also makes me question my own judgment for trusting in someone undeserving of my trust." Betrayal replaces your self-assurance with self-doubt and erodes your confidence, commitment, and energy.

As mentioned earlier, betrayals range in intensity. If you're not heavily invested in a relationship, being betrayed may cause you to feel unsettled, irked, or discouraged. When those in whom you've invested a great deal of yourself betray you, however, you may experience extreme emotions of shock, anger, alienation, inferiority, or worthlessness. One member of a telecommunications company reflected on being betrayed by his co-worker: "I had to get support from human resources. I asked for a transfer as soon as possible. I couldn't work with someone I didn't trust."

Betrayal is deeply felt—so much so that people use physical words to describe their emotional states after being betrayed.

They tell us they feel as if they've been "punched in the stomach" or "kicked in the teeth." A leader in a pharmaceutical company shared: "I really got beat up in that board meeting this morning. I felt betrayed by those who said they'd support my new ideas. I'm not sure I can trust any of them now."

Major Betrayals Diminish Your Capacity for Trust

When a trusted friend and colleague stole Sharon's creative idea for an ad campaign she'd been working on for months, the betrayal shook her deeply. A designer for a major advertising agency in New York City, Sharon became righteously enraged when her colleague received a large year-end bonus as a reward for her successful ad campaign. Sharon cut ties with her colleague and became extremely cautious about sharing her ideas with anyone.

A major betrayal, intentional or not, is shocking and devastating. What you thought was bedrock becomes shifting sand; what you thought to be true becomes false; what you thought permanent becomes impermanent. Your world turns upside down, and you may be tossed into emotional chaos. "My experience of betrayal is that I'm standing on a rug, and the rug is suddenly pulled out from under me. I'm tumbling helplessly out of control," a former client once told us.

Major betrayals are shocking and devastating, and they undermine your perceptions of yourself and others.

Betrayal can deeply wound your ability to trust everyone around you. When you suffer a major betrayal, you may find yourself wondering whom it's safe to trust. Or you may make a promise to yourself that you won't trust anyone. It's common to transfer your feelings to other relationships when trust breaks down. It's human nature to take betrayal personally. Even if you can forgive, you don't forget.

Betrayal can also impact your ability to trust yourself. Being left out of a significant decision that has implications on your work or life, being lied to about the status of an initiative, being passed up for a promotion you were led to believe was yours: these situations can all bring up feelings of worthlessness and may diminish your self-esteem and sense of confidence. You wind up feeling attacked, wounded, and vulnerable. You may question your value and self-worth, asking, "What is wrong with me that someone would treat me this way?" Betrayal deeply wounds your relationship with yourself and others—not just with your betrayer.

Minor Betrayals Test Your Capacity for Trust

Lou, an executive director, sat down with his employees to review how a plan to restructure the department would impact their roles and responsibilities. He discovered everyone had heard the news already. He felt betrayed that the person he'd confided in had breached his confidentiality.

Minor, everyday behaviors that break trust may seem small and subtle, but their impact is not. They accumulate over time and create a climate of distrust. They impact your commitment and ability to have confidence in your own and others' work. When you sense your colleagues' intentions and motives are not sincere or authentic, you may feel angry, helpless, and fearful. You may pull back, disengage, or become resentful—or even lose your ability to trust in general.

Minor betrayals can be most insidious because they often don't get addressed—yet they don't go unnoticed. These minor breaches of trust can create significant hurts, which lead to a state of major betrayals, particularly when their impact is chalked up to "just the way it is around here." Minor betrayals accumulate until one day people realize the extent to which they've been quietly misled and hurt through deception, dishonesty, or omission, and they head for the exit door on that relationship, job, or company. Or worse yet, they stay and join the ranks of the working wounded. They do as little as they can get away with.

Minor betrayals often go unaddressed—but they don't go unnoticed.

Most betrayals in the workplace are not intentionally malicious and are not designed to hurt others. They occur when people are overworked, overextended, stressed out, and trying to do more with less. When you allow others to get away with minor breaches of trust, however, it becomes easier for them to betray you in major ways. The cumulative effect of these betrayals damages your working relationships and eats away at your Capacity for Trust. You begin operating from a place of fear and worry about whether to trust others. Your behavior reflects this fear and influences how others approach you. Distrust breeds distrust and ultimately leads to more betrayal.

How You Betray Yourself

Most of us rarely set out to betray or let another person down. But we do. When you betray another, the first person you betray is yourself. You're vulnerable to betraying yourself when you overlook your own needs and fail to speak your truth.

You said yes to a request when you really wanted to say no or not now. You didn't request the additional support you needed to meet a deadline, so now you're working sixteen-hour days. You agreed to move the dates for a business trip knowing it would cut into precious family or weekend time. You agreed to a job assignment you knew you wouldn't enjoy because you wanted to be seen as serious about your career. After all, it was only for a year. That year turns into a very long year!

How Your Actions Lead to Self-Betrayal

When you agree to terms and conditions that you know are not mutually serving—that you know will come at your own expense—you override your needs and betray yourself. You may push beyond your physical limits and compromise self-care by working excessive hours, eating poorly, and skipping your exercise routine because you can't take the time for it. You say yes when you needed to say no. You become skillful at self-sacrifice to get your work done. You become pressed and anxious by simply trying to do too much. You put the job and others before yourself. You pay the price.

When you betray another, the first person you betray is yourself.

What causes people to override their core needs and be vulnerable to betraying themselves? The answer is fear: fear of not being good enough (*I have to do more*); fear of not being seen as competent (*I won't ask for help because then they'll be right*); fear of not being seen as cooperative (*I won't disagree with others' views*); fear of not being considered for promotion (*I'll take on the extra assignments to show them what I can do, even if it means I don't take a vacation this summer!*).

> *Darryl, an account manager, faced delivery deadlines and was rushing across town from one meeting to another. Trying to multitask by texting while driving, he had a near fatal car accident. While he recovered from his injuries, he felt the pain of self-betrayal, saying, "I was so fixated on doing my job, I forgot who I am. I am a father. How could I have been so irresponsible to my family? To myself?"*

When you override your personal needs and become anxious and overextended, you lose your center point, your sense of being grounded, and ultimately your sense of self. "I have been pushing so hard I can't feel myself anymore," said Claire, an interior designer, at completion of a major project.

When you're not aware of yourself, you aren't able to be aware of others. It's in this space of disconnection from yourself that you let others down. In your haste, pace, and ceaseless pushing, you lose your footing. When you have little compassion for yourself, you're unlikely to have compassion for others. You may unintentionally betray them because you have first betrayed yourself.

Fear causes you to be vulnerable to betraying yourself and others.

How Your Perceptions and Beliefs Lead to Self-Betrayal

Your Capacity for Trust influences your perceptions and beliefs, which in turn influences your readiness and willingness to trust (or betray) yourself and others. When your Capacity for Trust is constricted, you aren't as ready and willing to trust. This is when you are most vulnerable to disappointing, letting down, and betraying yourself and others. You may even expect to be disappointed as you lose faith that others will come through for you. The following questions illuminate how you may set yourself up for betrayal when you are not ready and willing to trust in others or yourself. Here, you see the natural impact of your orientation to the four questions presented in the previous chapter, "How You Trust."

Do You Expect to Be Rejected? If you expect to be rejected or criticized, you test people's loyalty and commitment to you. Rather than being open to what you might experience and expect the best, you presume the worst: *You'll have to prove to me that you're trustworthy first.* You find yourself on the defense, and you're ready to run from or beat up those individuals who may present a danger to your delicate sense of safety and identity. In this situation, trust may be a long time coming. If you're not willing to give it, you will not get it. Remember, trust begins with you.

Do You Contribute to Conflict? Your expectations of conflict generate the very conflict and distrust you fear. Your attitude influences your interactions with others. As a result of betrayal you may be inclined to enter a potentially challenging conversation on the defensive assuming the other person is not aligned with your interests and is looking to battle. You set yourself up to experience the very dynamic from which you are attempting to protect yourself. As one frontline factory worker said to a co-worker, "If you're looking for a fight, by golly I'm going to help you find one!"

Thought is creative. When you perceive others intend harm before you've examined your assumptions, you bring yourself to the relationship with judgment and criticism. You are on guard. When you're reluctant to trust in others, you behave in ways to protect yourself that cause others to react in a similar fashion. You may not give trust an opportunity to form.

Are You Preoccupied with Your Own Problems? When you are constantly preoccupied with your own problems, you may be totally unaware of your self-absorption and how it affects others. For example, if you're fostering an attitude that the world is treating you poorly, you rarely feel responsible for or sensitive to the pain you cause others. This preoccupation with yourself causes you to be unaware of your actions. As a result, you may break promises, miss deadlines, and be insensitive to the problems you create.

If you have a low Capacity for Trust in yourself, you may feel victimized by your circumstances and unresolved patterns of betrayal in your life. You may come across as needy, emotionally draining, and untrustworthy to your co-workers. Your preoccupation with the past causes you to be unaware of your actions and how you betray others. When problems are brought to your attention, you justify and rationalize your behavior.

Do You Create Difficulty Unnecessarily? If you're preoccupied with a frantic search for certainty and predictability, you may be unable to understand the complex dynamics of trust-based relationships. You may have little tolerance for differences in others, and you may come across as self-righteous, speak in absolutes, and think in simplistic, black-or-white, good-or-bad terms. If you disagree or don't understand something, you may react with a verbal attack. You assume the worst and treat your assumption as fact. You may regard life as a battle to be won, and your goal is being right and winning at all costs. If so, you have a limited ability to deal with the uncertainty of new situations. For example, when facilitating a team meeting, you might come across as domineering: *My way is the right way, trust me.* You may have difficulty leading an open-ended dialogue session that lacks formal structure.

The need to be always right and win at all costs creates distrust and limits your overall effectiveness.

Do You Discount People? If you feel hurt, embarrassed, or frightened in your association with someone, you may conjure up an elaborate mental smoke screen to protect yourself from memories triggered by past painful experiences. By devaluing others, you're able to distance yourself from them. History has shown that in war, countries discount other nations or ethnic groups by labeling them as the enemy and portraying them in nonhuman, demeaning terms. It's easier to drop a bomb on your enemies if you convince yourself they're evil.

In the workplace, if you foster this perspective, you may not be able to distinguish individuals from the groups to which they belong and prejudge them without fully understanding them. When your Capacity for Trust is contracted, and you are unaware of this contraction, you're positioned to fail in your cooperation with others. You're perceived as difficult to work with, and others are disinclined to readily share information and resources to accomplish the job. You are not invited into collaboration. Your working relationships suffer, and you and the organization are cheated of your potential performance. You lose out on what others have to bring to you.

Betrayal Can Be a Teacher if You Let It

Betrayal happens every day. It's a natural part of human relationships and can be a gift and a teacher if you allow it to be. You don't have control over how others treat you. You *do* have control over how you choose to respond. You can choose to be a victim who is lost in anger, bitterness, and resentment. You can let your Capacity for Trust in yourself and others contract and shut yourself off from healthy ways of relating. Or you can choose to step into and work through your pain on a quest for meaning, insight, and wholeness. Choosing to embrace betrayal and to work through the pain will strengthen and deepen your understanding of yourself and your relationships.

Betrayal can be a gift and a teacher if you allow it to be.

Knowing how to deal with betrayal is essential to maintaining healthy levels of trust in your relationships. Equipped with the tools we give you in the next chapter, you'll learn how to trust again—and help others to do so as well. The insights you gain will support you in all aspects of your life, both at work and at home.

Trust Building in Action
Reflecting on Your Experience

1. Reflect on a time in your life when you felt let down, hurt, disappointed, or betrayed, intentionally or unintentionally: What happened? How did you feel—emotionally, psychologically, and spiritually—when it happened to you? How did you respond to the experience? What short-term and long-term impact did it have on you?

2. Reflect on a time when someone felt betrayed by you. What happened? What impact did your behavior had on them? How did you respond to their reactions of your betrayal? What did you learn about yourself and relationships?

Trust Tip ▶ *In order to fully understand trust, you must understand betrayal. Betrayal is a natural part of human relationships. Critical to the health of your relationships is how you choose to respond to betrayal when it happens.*

CHAPTER EIGHT

How Trust Is Rebuilt: Seven Steps for Healing

The Promise of Renewal

Chest aching, stomach churning, Roberta splashed water on her face as she fought back tears of shock, horror, and deep hurt. She could not believe what she'd just heard. She honestly thought she and Daniel were totally aligned. What a way to find out they weren't!

The company president had given Roberta the responsibility of overseeing the design and development of a major building complex. Roberta had asked Daniel to work with her on developing the proposal outlining the approach to the project. She had tremendous respect for Daniel's skill and talent, and they had worked well together in the past.

Roberta felt that she and Daniel had developed a solid proposal and looked forward to reviewing it with the president. At the start of the review meeting, she could not believe her ears when the president mentioned that Daniel had stopped into his office that morning—behind Roberta's back—and announced that he had major concerns about the proposal and about Roberta's ability to oversee the project. Roberta was flabbergasted.

Trust is always vulnerable, even in high-trust relationships. Letdowns, hurts, and betrayals simply come with the territory of opening ourselves up to other people. The disappointments we experience in these partnerships can cut deep and knock us off our feet—or they can seem more like blips on the radar of "business as usual." No matter the severity, however, all betrayals have the potential to accumulate into confidence-busting, commitment-breaking, and energy-draining patterns.

Few of us know how to deal with the emotional pain of broken trust because our culture doesn't encourage reflection and genuine expression of our feelings. Yet, the impact of unresolved breaches of trust can be devastating to people's health, careers, and personal relationships. When we wrote the first and second editions of *Trust and Betrayal in the Workplace*, we received tremendous feedback from our readers, asking for more detail and direction on each of the Seven Steps for Healing to rebuild trust. Recognizing that people needed and wanted to deal with their betrayals—big and small—and proactively work through them, we wrote an entire book on the steps, which we call *Rebuilding Trust in the Workplace: Seven Steps to Renew Confidence, Commitment, and Energy*. The chapter you're about to read is an overview of our steps for renewing trust. For more detail about each of the steps, we invite you to read our second book.

The framework we provide in this chapter—and in *Rebuilding Trust in the Workplace*—will help you learn to trust again with compassion and courage, and help you respond to others appropriately when you've let them down.

Betrayal is universal. If it hasn't happened already, at some point in your life you'll be called upon to support a friend, colleague, or loved one whose trust has been broken. Embracing the Seven Steps will enable you to lead others through their hurt, disappointment, and pain toward a place of renewed trust—both in others and in themselves. This renewal can happen on an individual basis, within your team, or across your organization. You can use the steps at home, in your church, or within your volunteer groups. The Seven Steps are just as powerful and universal as betrayal itself.

You Have a Choice

You want trusting relationships. You want to grow, understand, and be able to move through hurts to a place of hope and confidence. Yet, you struggle with how to get there. How do you deal with disappointment and betrayal? How do you make sense of what happened? How do you learn to trust again?

Your journey toward renewed trust begins with you and your choice about how you respond when your trust has been broken. Whether you've been betrayed intentionally or unintentionally, you may feel helpless and hopeless. You may feel as though you have no control over what was "done to you." It's true that you don't have control over what others do. You *do*, however, have control over how you *choose* to respond. Imagine that you're hiking in the woods and you come to a fork in the trail. A sign gives you the option to go down the path of anger, bitterness, and resentment, or you can take the path of healing, optimism, and renewal. The path you take is up to you. How do you want to move forward—mired in patterns of energy-draining distrust or buoyed by awareness and compassion?

> ***You can't control what others do to you.***
> ***You can control how you choose to respond.***

When you choose to hold onto betrayal with clenched fists, you become the victim of your experience and shut yourself off from the opportunities that rebuilding trust provides. You miss out on the insights, the lessons, and the chance to transform your experience in your own head and heart. Instead of healing, you become consumed by what someone "did to you" and allow another's actions to eat away at your spirit and self-confidence.

Alternatively, when you choose to embrace the pain of betrayal with courage and compassion, you embark on a journey of renewal in which you replace anger with restored belief in yourself and faith in the spirit of human relationships. You learn to understand your hurts and work through them. You may even ask yourself if you contributed in some way to what occurred—an honesty that's rewarded with deepened respect for yourself and your future relationships. You learn to trust again, and you feel whole.

The Seven Steps for Healing help you move through your pain and reframe your experience of betrayal with compassion and forgiveness. You allow betrayal to teach you about yourself, about your relationships, and about life in general. You become empowered to let go of your fear, doubt, and insecurity in order to reclaim your boundless energy, potential, and creativity. You open yourself—heart and mind—to what still *can* be rather than remaining shackled to thoughts of what *should* have been.

Whether you are feeling betrayed, coming to terms with having betrayed another, or simply trying to help others through their hurts, the Seven Steps will help you realize the renewal and peace of mind you and others seek.

Seven Steps for Healing

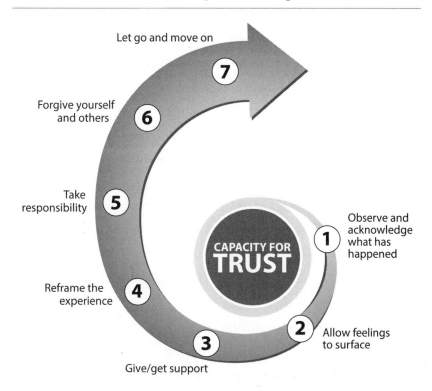

The Seven Steps for Healing

The Seven Steps for Healing are not simply an academic theory. They are tested, proven, and universal. The steps emerged out of Dennis's own experience with some of the most basic sources of betrayal: broken promises, dishonesty, and abandonment.

> *"My world came crashing down," Dennis shared. "I came back from a four-day doctorate research session and discovered that my wife had been having an affair with a co-worker for six months. I was stunned, confused, and disoriented. I was angry and upset. But most of all, I questioned myself. How could I not have noticed?*

I loved my wife and our two little boys. For the year and a half after discovering the affair, I did whatever I could to hold the marriage together. I went to counseling to work through my issues and the pain of my failing marriage, but my wife was not willing to join me in this effort.

We worked out an amicable divorce agreement and were awarded joint custody of our boys. Although I had my boys on alternating weekends as well as some holidays and vacations, I lost the life with them I had cherished.

A very painful part of the early years after the divorce were my long, sad rides home after dropping the boys off after their weekends with me. I cried so hard I often had to pull over to the side of the road because I couldn't see straight enough to drive.

This intense pain continued for quite some time before subsiding. What I was grieving was the loss of my daily life with my family, the loss of what could have been but would never be. I missed tucking the boys into bed every night and rubbing their backs as they dozed off to sleep. I missed making them breakfast and putting them on the school bus.

In my grieving, I needed to allow my feelings to surface, to release my anger, my hurt, and my deep pain. And I did, again and again. Although living this chapter of my life was a nightmare, years later I was able to see its enormously redeeming value. A powerful lesson for me was that although I felt victimized, I certainly did not need to remain a victim. I chose to work through my pain and learned a lot about myself. I became more sensitive to others in pain and discovered how I could help them heal.

Through my healing I was eventually led to my future wife—and business partner—Michelle. Together, we developed the trust-based work that we do today. And my healing gave birth to the framework of these Seven Steps for Healing."

As Dennis worked hard to understand the reasons why bad things happened to him, integrate this awareness into his life, and forgive himself and his betrayer, he was able to let go and move on. He released his energies from dwelling on the negative impacts of the betrayal itself and was able to nurture a deeper grasp of the intrinsic nature of trust, a seed that eventually evolved into the Seven Steps for Healing.

The steps are intended to help you work through the painful feelings you experience when your trust has been broken and help you move toward renewal. Although they're numbered sequentially, you don't necessarily work through them in a linear fashion. You may be in multiple steps at the same time, or you may have completed one step and moved on to the next, only to re-experience aspects of an earlier step. Feelings come in waves while working the Seven Steps; there are highs and lows, ebbs and flows—yet there is overall movement toward renewal and restored trust in yourself and your relationships.

Each of the Seven Steps represents a phase of the process that can be applied to rebuilding trust on the individual, team, and organizational levels. For teams and organizations to recover from betrayal, individuals need to heal first—though eventually, renewal needs to occur at all levels and in every corner of your workplace. You have a part to play in that healing. Rebuilding trust is a choice. Rebuilding trust begins with you.

Step 1: Observe and Acknowledge What Has Happened

"I couldn't ignore what had happened," said James, a mechanical engineer. "In spite of the fact that I wanted to run away from it all and just work harder and harder, I couldn't ignore the deep pain I was feeling. It was as if someone had punched me in the gut and ripped out my insides. I was hurting, I was angry, and I hated my co-worker for stealing credit for work I had done and then lying about it to make me wrong."

Moving through the pain of a breach of trust or betrayal to renewal starts with self-discovery and awareness. It's important that you take time to acknowledge what happened to you and its impact. What behaviors led to the betrayal? What impact is the betrayal having on you—on your daily life both at work and at home? What did you lose when your trust was broken?

Acknowledging the details of betrayal is the first step toward rebuilding trust. After all, you can't heal what you can't see. In this first step, you benefit from mustering the courage to look at your experience honestly; consciously observing its silhouette and impact, almost as if from the outside. From this perspective, you don't judge your reactions—or ignore or deny them. You allow them. You pay attention to the sources of your pain and ask questions about the feelings they evoke. You hush your inner critic, lift your mind into a neutral zone, and tap the wellspring of your inner perspectives and emotions. You don't need to probe too deeply to understand or analyze your thoughts or feelings in this first step. You simply need to acknowledge that they exist, recognize their impact, and prepare yourself to begin addressing them.

*Acknowledging betrayal and its impact is the
first step toward rebuilding trust.*

Step 2: Allow Feelings to Surface

*"I was livid!" said Maureen, a stylist, in a trendy salon. "I
hated the person for what she'd done to me, and I hated
myself for being so naive that I didn't see it coming. I couldn't
sleep, couldn't eat, my stomach was in knots, my head was
throbbing—I ached all over. All I wanted to do was wallow in
self-pity. 'Why me?' I said. 'I didn't deserve this!' "*

When you've been betrayed, you hurt. You feel drained from
the emotional upheaval the betrayal creates in your life. It's vital
you dig down and give yourself permission to feel your hurt—
all of it. When you respect your pain, you honor yourself and
your perceptions of your experience. Those perceptions and the
feelings they generate are valid and deserve to be recognized.
You may feel distracted, uncomfortable, or unsettled. Or you
may be devastated, horrified, or depressed. You may feel a bit
uptight, or you may struggle to suppress your rage. Regardless
of their intensity, the only way to work through your emotions is
to acknowledge them. Only *then* can you begin to release them
with compassion.

Unfortunately, no one else can do this work for you. Betrayal
robs you of your time, your energy, and possibly your opportunities and hopes for the future. You need to grieve this loss. You may
be able to delegate other tasks in your life, but grieving isn't one
of them. This is your work. The only effective way to experience

true renewal is to work through your grief. But take heart: for those willing to embrace their emotions, there is a light at the end of the tunnel. Renewal awaits you. Healing provides deeper value and meaning to the pain you are experiencing, though that may be hard for you to believe while you're in it.

You may be able to delegate other tasks in your life, but grieving isn't one of them.

You may find that you need to create quiet time alone to get in touch with your feelings. Or perhaps physical exercise or writing in a journal would be more helpful. What's important is not what you do but *how* you do it. Choose an activity that helps you get in touch with your feelings rather than escape and avoid them.

In releasing your emotions, you must also release your guilt. An act of betrayal may occur only once, but you may relive it in your mind a thousand times. If you're hard on yourself, you become riddled with guilt over what you did, or you may or replay over and over again the injustice you suffered. By doing so, you hurt yourself even more. Although it's important to feel in order to grieve, guilt and worry are not helpful emotions for restoring broken trust. They drain your energy, cloud your thinking, and clutter your emotions. Let them go.

Step 3: Get Support

"I need help! I can't go on trying to do my job as if nothing happened, feeling like this," Trent, an accountant, said. "I need to talk with someone—someone I trust—which isn't too many people these days. I can't confide in my co-worker Tammy;

she would blab it all over the department. I can't go to my supervisor, Tom; he may use it against me in my performance review. Who can I rely on that I can have confidence in? Maybe I should look for help outside the organization, maybe a coach or counselor."

Moving through betrayal is difficult to do alone. You need support to help you fully observe and acknowledge what happened, to allow your feelings to surface, and to understand them. Yet it may be difficult for you to reach out and ask for help. When you've been deeply hurt, you feel vulnerable, and your instinct may be to draw back.

Although it's understandable you'd be reluctant to seek out help, this is the time to be kind to yourself. You don't need to go through this painful journey alone. You can turn to a colleague, friend, or family member. You can connect with a counselor, member of the clergy, or professional coach. You may feel safer talking with a loved one who knows you very well, or you may prefer hearing the thoughts of a neutral third party.

Regardless of whom you ask for help, remember that the role of your supporter isn't to judge, criticize, or help you heap blame on your betrayer. Although those actions may seem attractive in the short term, they'll only trap you in your pain and throw up obstacles on your path to restored trust. The best confidants provide you with perspective and help you gain a more nuanced understanding of your experience. They help you recognize what you're feeling and thinking, and lead the way to uncovering the betrayal's deeper lessons. It's not always easy to receive these insights, but not hearing them may lead to more significant hurts in the future as your trust continues to unravel.

The best supporters provide you with perspective.

Your supporter can also help you create clarity around your needs and desires, refine your expectations of others' abilities to meet those wishes, and ultimately view your experience—and your betrayer—with compassion. You can work together to recognize the choices you have in moving forward after the betrayal and consider the ramifications of those choices. Remember, although you cannot change others' behaviors, you can choose how to respond.

Step 4: Reframe the Experience

> *"Why did this happen to me? What circumstances led to this betrayal? What messages do I need to hear at this time in my life? What lessons do I need to learn?" thought James after hearing his co-worker had taken credit for his hard work.*

When you reframe your perspective on betrayal, you're able to transform it from a trauma to an opportunity for learning and growth. Instead of locking the experience into a hurtful place in your mind that drains your self-confidence, you allow your curiosity to take root and open yourself to imagining the bigger picture at play in your relationships—and in your life. Your hurt and pain become stepping-stones to renewal and a deepened Capacity for Trust.

To begin reframing your experience, place it in a larger context. Think about the circumstances that surrounded your betrayal—both those within your control and those outside your control. Shift your focus from one of defeat and victimhood to one of proactive understanding. Ask yourself guiding questions that will help you see the betrayal differently; see why it has power

Reframe the Experience

Rebuilding trust is a journey of inquiry. Asking these reframing questions will enable you to make meaning out of what you experienced.

- Why did this happen? What extenuating circumstances might be at play? Is there something I might not be aware of?

- How can I change my viewpoint in order to gain perspective?

- Might I be blowing this out of proportion? Might my current pain stem from unresolved hurts in my past?

- What might the other person have been experiencing in his or her own life that influenced his or her behavior?

- What can I reference about the past—the good times of our relationships—that can help me have compassion for my betrayer?

- What options do I have for responding to this situation differently?

- What can I take from this experience? What lessons do I need to learn?

- What is the purpose of this event in my life at this point?

over you. Take yourself to a place of stillness. Listen to your inner voice; it knows how to answer these questions through the lens of compassion, if you let it.

Reflecting on these questions helps you sort out your thoughts and emotions and arrive at greater insight. As you reframe your experience, you gain wisdom, inner strength, and resilience. You begin to see life's experiences as opportunities to transform your understanding of yourself and those around you. And you receive new trust in your ability to overcome life's challenges. Remember, that which doesn't kill you makes you stronger!

Step 5: Take Responsibility

"What was my role in this experience?" Marjorie, a staff
trainer, asked herself. "What did I do or not do that contrib-
uted to this betrayal? What could I have done differently?"

When you're in pain, it's normal to project your feelings onto others; to lay blame and step away from responsibility. In order to rebuild trust, however, it's important you take ownership of your role in a betrayal and consider the choices you made that may have contributed to it. This might be hard to do. After feeling betrayed, you may want to point your finger or get revenge. Although understandable, there's simply no benefit to this perspective.

When you allow yourself to continue patterns of justifying, defending, and explaining your own behaviors in your relationships, you begin to take others' trust in you for granted. Even if you're not at fault in a given situation, others need to see— and *you* need to see—that you're willing to do what it takes to learn from a situation and move forward in a stronger way. The moment you stop showing up with this level of humble commitment is the moment you lose trust—both in yourself and with others.

So rather than dwelling on who's at fault, you'll find greater energy in pinpointing which behaviors to practice moving forward. You may be partially at fault for the betrayal, you may be fully responsible, or you may be completely innocent. Regardless of how you did or didn't contribute to a breakdown of trust, you *are* responsible for your response to it. Only you can stem the energy drain that holding onto betrayal creates in your life. The choices you make today create your tomorrow.

Take Responsibility

When you accept responsibility for your behaviors and choices, you're in a better position to examine what led up to the break down in trust and how you may have contributed to it. You may ask yourself:

- What role did I play in the process?
- What did I do or not do that contributed to the betrayal?
- Am I owning or disowning my part?
- Am I making excuses or diverting blame away from myself?
- Do I have a need to make the other person wrong?
- What could I have done differently?
- What can I do now to take charge of the situation?

You have choices in any situation, even when you are hurting.

Step 6: Forgive Yourself and Others

"I need to forgive myself—mostly for being so naive," said Cynthia, a young intern. "I was working hard and doing all I could to keep up, and I was blindsided. Now I know better. I may forgive George because carrying the anger is wearing me down. But I will never forget the lessons I have learned—nor should I. They are too darn valuable to forget."

Forgiveness is a gift you give yourself. When you don't forgive, you cling to your anger, resentment, and bitterness like a security blanket. You close off your heart, deplete your spirit, and interfere with your trustworthiness. You bring yourself to your relationships with fear and prejudgment and create the very circumstances in which betrayal can thrive. Learning to forgive releases you from this pattern of behavior and allows you to approach others with compassion and understanding.

The first step to being able to forgive others is to learn to forgive yourself when you betray them. Breaking trust doesn't mean you're a bad person. Most of the time you slip up because you're rushing around, trying to do more with less time, energy, and money. The more self-aware and compassionate you are, however, the more you feel the pain you cause others, and the more you need to forgive yourself when you stumble. Forgiving yourself is a gift you give others, too.

The first step to forgiving others is to learn to forgive yourself.

Not everyone sees forgiveness this way. Some view it as letting people off the hook. With a major betrayal, sometimes people hurt so much they hate their betrayer and want them to hurt as much as they do. They want to get back. They want to get even. With a minor betrayal, people simply may not have the energy to wish the other person well. Though none of us wants to admit it, when you hate, it is extremely difficult to heal. To shift from hate to healing, it's important that you shift your focus from your betrayer to your wounded self, that you detach from the person who hurt you in order to let go. It's important to essentially *choose* yourself, so you can begin to recover.

When you forgive you're able to heal more rapidly. You no longer hold yourself hostage, waiting for an apology from the person who betrayed you. An apology may certainly be warranted and may support your healing, but you can move through the Seven Steps in the absence of it, if you choose.

When Michelle's father, Jack, was seventeen, he enlisted in the army and was sent to fight in the Korean War. Months later, Michelle's grandparents received the telegram everyone lived in fear of receiving—their son was missing in action. They later learned that Jack was alive, but had been taken prisoner by the Chinese in Northern Korea.

Korea is one of the coldest places on the planet. Temperatures reach minus 40 degrees in the winter. The captives of war lived in huts with dirt floors within the prison compound. The men had louse-ridden mattresses and blankets. At night, they lined the interior of the huts like sardines and slept close together for warmth. They wore thin sneakers made from canvas. Each prisoner got one bowl of maggot-infested porridge twice a day, morning and evening.

In those conditions, people do things they wouldn't ordinarily do. In the middle of the night, some prisoners would die. When morning came, the living prisoners would prop up the dead and huddle close to them so it looked like everyone was there and accounted for. For the living, that meant an extra bit of porridge to share.

One day, Michelle's father ripped the corners of his tattered blanket and put them into the tips of his threadbare canvas sneakers so his frostbitten toes would have some warmth. He tucked the ends of the blanket back into the cot so no one would see the torn corners. The next morning during inspection, a prison guard came directly over to Jack's cot and pulled out the blanket. Jack was brought to the camp commander for interrogation. He stood up to him and fought back. He said they weren't following the Geneva Convention and men should not have to go to such extremes to stay alive. They said he had destroyed government property and would be punished.

And punished he was. They put Jack in a cell dug six feet into the ground. It was cold, dark, and damp. They kept him in that hole for ninety bitter cold days. When Jack came out, he learned that the Chinese had discovered the torn blanket because a fellow American soldier snitched on him for an extra bowl of porridge.

After close to three years held in captivity, the war ended and Jack was returned to American custody. Only 57 of the 363 men in his battalion survived. Jack weighed 78 pounds and was severely ill, barely hanging on to life. He was hospitalized for six months before being allowed to go home.

Later, when Jack had returned to active duty with the army, he was asked to testify in a court-marshal hearing of the man who had betrayed him. He said he would do so if ordered, but respectfully asked not to. With some distance, Michelle's father could feel compassion for and forgive the man who had betrayed him. Jack came to understand that in his suffering, the man first sold himself out before he betrayed Jack.

With compassion, you can choose to look at your betrayer differently. You can see him as a person who is struggling in his own pain. You may offer him benefit of the doubt: Is it possible that he lost his sense of himself? Is it possible he betrayed himself in the process of betraying me?

When you can do this, you're able to see those who betray you as people with needs, feelings, and vulnerabilities rather than demonizing them as evildoers from the dark side. When it comes right down to it, we are like our betrayers and they are like us. Your betrayer may have been stressed and up against a wall. Maybe she was doing the best she could and simply lost her footing, just as we all have many times. Forgiveness doesn't mean you condone the betrayal. Forgiveness just means you understand it.

The next step in healing occurs when you invite the person who betrayed you back into your life. You both have to be willing to come together and listen to each other, and the betrayer needs to be ready and willing to acknowledge and honestly apologize for what happened. You need your betrayers to understand the depth of the pain you suffered and make new promises he or she intends to keep.

If, however, the person who hurt you isn't ready or willing to talk with you openly, you still can heal within yourself. How do you know forgiveness has occurred? When you can think about people who betrayed you and wish them well, and feel gratitude for the lessons you learned from the experience.

Step 7: Let Go and Move On

"It's time to let go and move on," said Rosa, an experienced chef. "I've learned some lessons—difficult as they were to come by. I've spent enough time, energy, and emotion on this experience for a lifetime. I wouldn't want to go through this again, but I'm grateful for the experience and the lessons it provided me. It has strengthened me, and I'm glad it's over!"

The process of forgiving, letting go, and moving on is the final step in restoring your Capacity for Trust. How do you know you're ready to let go? When you're able to reflect on the betrayal and experience inner peace. Yes, you may still recall the pain, but you're able to claim a deeper sense of its role in your life.

In this final stage of the Seven Steps, it's helpful to look back over your experience, reflect on what you learned, and think about what you can carry with you into the future. How will you behave differently the next time? How will you continue to build trust?

You can always choose to act differently in the quest to build more trustworthy relationships. Like picking up any new skill, learning to relate to yourself or others in different ways with heightened awareness takes practice, time, and patience. Start with small steps. Experiment with new behaviors and see what works. Focus on what is in your power to control. Trust in yourself and in your newfound awareness of compassion and courage.

As you let go and move forward, you benefit from the increased energy that arises from focusing on the present. We all spend so much time thinking about the future—the mountain of tasks, projects, and big decisions that will get us to where we want to be. We often forget to reflect on what kind of person we want to *be* along our journey and once we arrive. As you tidy up the remnants of your passage through the Seven Steps, remember: trust begins with you.

We spend so much time focusing on the future that we often forget who we want to be along the way.

The Seven Steps Help You Heal

Going through the pain of betrayal and rebuilding trust in yourself and your co-workers takes a lot of hard work, courage, and compassion. Healing is neither spontaneous nor swift. The process of forgiving, letting go, and moving on, however, realigns you with your sense of self. By being more fully aware of who you are, you expand your Capacity for Trust in yourself and in others, and reap the benefits of the boundless energy that renewed trust brings.

Each of us works through the Seven Steps in our own way. Some of us need to spend more time on some steps than on others. Remember, intense feelings come in waves, so you may progress through several steps only to go back to earlier steps as additional feelings surface. Working through one experience may kick up the pain from previous experiences, and you may need to work on multiple steps at once. The order you work through the steps isn't important. What's important is that you, in your own way, go through the entire process with honesty and integrity.

By facing betrayal in a conscious way, you can move toward greater understanding of the value of your experience and develop a greater Capacity for Trust in yourself and in others. Only in this way can you find value and meaning in your pain and enrich your relationships in the future. Only in this way can you embrace the gifts that rebuilding trust offers.

Trust Building in Action

Reflecting on Your Experience

1. Think about the last time you were betrayed. Can you see ways that you contributed to this breach of trust?
2. Think about a time when you let down someone else. How did you deal with the impact of your actions?
   - What needs to happen for forgiveness to take place?
   - What do you need the most in order to rebuild trust?
   - What do you think the person you betrayed most needs from you?

Trust Tip ▶ *Life's most painful experiences provide life's most powerful lessons if you are willing to look, listen, and learn! The choices you make today create your tomorrow.*

CHAPTER NINE

How Trust Is Transformed: Transformative Trust

How do you create an abundance of trust in your life? How do you help your team and your organization take trust to the next level, even during periods of change when there are more questions than answers, when there are disappointments and uncertainty?

Faced with a strategic business decision handed down from corporate headquarters, one division of a Fortune 100 company had to lay off 100 people from its 420-person operation in a one-company rural town. The layoffs meant the most significant changes in the ten-year history of the division. Everyone in the community would feel the impact.

Although the local managers were not involved in the initial decision to reduce the division's workforce, they were fully responsible for implementing the change. They were committed to doing so in a way that honored their people, their contributions to the company, and the relationships they had developed with one another.

The local managers carefully orchestrated each phase of the downsizing process.

These leaders were sensitive to their employees' needs and acknowledged the impact of this change on both those who were leaving and those who would remain. "We know this is affecting your lives dramatically," the division manager said, holding back tears, but allowing himself to express his emotions. To ensure people remained fully informed, management opened lines of communication and held special meetings and forums every step of the way to make sure everyone heard the same message at the same time in person. They made sure that everyone had a safe place to talk about each piece of news after they received it.

Managers worked diligently to assist employees throughout the process, whether they were directly or indirectly affected. They set up career counseling and outplacement centers, visited with management in other organizations to explore job opportunities for those who were leaving, and invited companies into the plant to meet with job candidates. Venues were established to support those who weren't leaving the company. Skilled facilitators helped address transitional needs and set up closure meetings for employees to say good-bye to those who were leaving.

Within five months, management made sure that all the displaced employees who wanted to continue to work were placed in new jobs, inside or outside the corporation. They held open discussions with those remaining on how the layoffs affected them, their working relationships, and their performance. They clarified new sets of expectations and boundaries. Working with the employees, management formed agreements regarding new processes and relationships, established channels of communication and information sharing, and provided training to teach new skills.

Throughout this traumatic time in this company's history, the behaviors of the local managers cultivated Transformative Trust. Their conviction to honor their roles as leaders, their courage to tell the "hard" truth at all times, their compassion in remaining sensitive to the impact of the change on people's lives, and their awareness of the organizational community made a difference. People were able to cultivate trust even within an adverse situation because they demonstrated awareness of and caring about how others were affected by the experience.

Creating Transformative Trust

You've learned that trust begins with you: *you have to give it to get it.* When you consciously and consistently practice the behaviors of The Three Cs to lay a foundation of trust—and work through the Seven Steps for Healing to restore trust when it's been broken—you contribute to a workplace that cultivates Transformative Trust. You trust others more. They trust you more. You trust yourself more. This elevated level of trust energizes relationships and allows teams and organizations to function at their highest levels.

Transformative Trust is created when the level of trust among co-workers reaches a tipping point and begins to increase exponentially. At this moment, trust becomes self-generating and synergistic, and it takes on a dynamic force of its own. It becomes integrated into the way people interact and do business every day. When the level of trust reaches this critical threshold, it transforms the ways by which you and your teammates work together and expands what you're able to accomplish. Transformative Trust changes you, your life, and the lives of others in your organization.

> ### Transformative Trust energizes relationships and expands what you are able to accomplish.

Transformative Trust is a game changer. Trustworthiness becomes an asset that takes your relationships to the next level. You feel good about yourself, your relationships, and your shared work. You feel inspired about others' belief in you and what you're accomplishing. You feel acknowledged and respected, and you strive to ensure others feel acknowledged and respected. You are guided by intentions to be in the highest, best service to one another. As a result, you and those you work with show up for work alert, excited, and full of energy, knowing that what you do makes a positive difference.

> *Victor, a technician, knew his news wouldn't make Pam happy, but he also knew he had to share it with her directly. She had already emphasized she needed the lab report by this afternoon. The problem? Equipment failure (again). Victor knew it was going to take many hours before he could complete the required tests.*
>
> *Pam listened as Victor outlined the issues and waited until he finished before she spoke. "Victor, thanks for alerting me to this issue. Let's focus on what can be done to get this work completed on time. Did you know that the biochemistry department at another hospital in our area health service region just purchased a new machine? Let's call them to see whether they can help out."*
>
> *Victor felt affirmed in his decision to discuss the delay with Pam before the deadline arrived. Pam smiled. She'd noticed that Victor had certainly started to practice the*

behaviors promoted at the last team meeting, namely to remember to "renegotiate directly with the requestor" when one cannot honor a commitment.

In work environments where Transformative Trust unfolds, you and your co-workers learn to communicate openly and honestly with one another, even if you need to share bad news. You give one another the benefit of the doubt, take responsibility to keep your agreements, and renegotiate if you need more time or help. You learn to manage your fears, test your assumptions, avoid prejudgment, and resist getting defensive. You redirect tendencies to judge and criticize your co-workers into a desire to understand their experiences and needs. You become more willing to trust in your relationships within your team and across the organization.

It's important to remember the presence of Transformative Trust does not mean breaches of trust don't occur. There will always be disappointments, letdowns, and occasions of broken trust. These hurts simply come with the territory of relationships. The presence of this form of trust does mean that you and the people you work with are committed to minimizing the common breaches of trust and practicing the Seven Steps when betrayals happen. You make conscious choices to treat betrayals as opportunities to strengthen interpersonal relationships, team and organizational effectiveness, and overall efficiency.

Transformative Trust doesn't mean betrayals don't happen. It means you and others are willing to work together to overcome them.

An organization rich in Transformative Trust is the antithesis of one mired in the impacts of betrayal. Betrayal and distrust come from a place of deprivation and scarcity, whereas Transformative Trust comes from a place of abundance. When you and those you work with honor, respect, nurture, and trust one another, your Capacity for Trust flourishes and you unhook the bounds on what you're able to accomplish together through fruitful collaboration, innovation, and problem solving.

The Four Catalysts for Building Transformative Trust

Although the development of Transformative Trust is simple to discuss, you have to dig deep to create it. Consistently practicing the behaviors of the Three Dimensions of Trust—The Three Cs of Trust—and working through the Seven Steps for Healing requires conscious effort. To help you get farther faster in your journey to build Transformative Trust, we've identified four catalysts that amplify your trust building efforts: Conviction, Courage, Compassion, and Community. We call these catalysts The Four Cs.

Conviction helps you practice the behaviors that build Trust of Character, Trust of Communication, and Trust of Capability day in and day out. Courage allows you to honor yourself and your relationships when the going gets tough. Compassion enables you to forgive yourself and others for letdowns, mistakes, and transgressions. And a sense of Community encourages you to reframe painful situations, take responsibility for your behaviors, and look at the bigger picture to see your contribution to others. The Four Cs help you move yourself, your colleagues, and your organization beyond betrayal toward an enduring culture of Transformative Trust. Trust begins with you.

We use the word *expansion* to visualize the interplay of The Three Cs of Trust, the Seven Steps for Healing, and the catalysts

Transformative Trust

CONSISTENT PRACTICE OF TRUST BUILDING BEHAVIORS TRANSFORMS TRUST
Self-Generating, Increases Exponentially, Energy-Producing

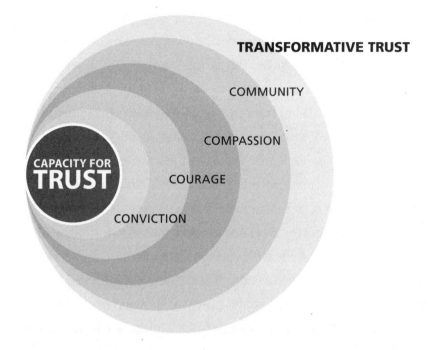

that create Transformative Trust. (Please refer to the Seven Steps for Healing figure in Chapter 8.) Consciously practicing the behaviors of The Three Cs of Trust and the Seven Steps for Healing expands your own and your colleagues' capacities to trust in yourself and in your relationships, team, organization, and surrounding stakeholders. Taking the next step and tapping the catalysts of Transformative Trust—The Four Cs—amplifies your collective trust building behaviors within the Three Dimensions of Trust and the healing steps. This amplification creates momentum in the outward expansion of trust in your organization, giving rise to a multiplier effect that eventually leads trust to increase exponentially and synergistically.

When you and your colleagues fail to practice trust building behaviors, work through breached trust, and develop your relationships using The Four Cs of Transformative Trust, this expansion of trust reverses. Your collective Capacity for Trust depletes, relationships de-energize, confidence dwindles, and commitment wanes. Bottom-line results reflect this contraction. Conversely, when there is a conscious practice of trust building behaviors, the steps to rebuild trust are honored, and The Four Cs are integrated into how you and your co-workers relate to one another, your Capacity for Trust expands. Relationships are energized, confidence surges, and commitment skyrockets. Bottom-line results become a source of organizational pride.

Building Transformative Trust is everyone's responsibility, but it begins with you. It begins with your positive intention and personal commitment to be aware of yourself and your colleagues and to integrate trust building strategies into how you show up every day. This work requires discipline. The catalysts we explore will help you stay on track when you're challenged, confused, or simply depleted from your efforts. Digging deep to tap into your inner conviction, courage, compassion, and sense of community will unlock profound sources of energy and enable you to approach your workplace relationships with renewed vigor. Trust is generated within you and your relationships with others. Trust begins with you.

Conviction

Your convictions stem from your awareness of your higher purpose—your grasp of what is most meaningful to you and your desire to make a contribution to others. You live by your convictions when you're authentic in your words and actions, have passion for what you do, and maintain confidence in what you believe. This alignment between intention and action strengthens your ability to trust yourself in challenging situations. Moreover, it encourages others to trust that you're committed to making your convictions a reality.

Your convictions stem from your awareness of your higher purpose.

Unfortunately, in some work environments, authenticity is punished. In such a workplace, it may be tempting to bow to pressure and "go underground" with your inner truth. When you don't listen to your own voice, trust your instincts, and hold firm to what you know is right, however, you betray yourself and invite distrust from others. You run the risk of being seen as inauthentic or self-serving, as just going through the motions, or even as taking advantage of others by taking more than you give. When others see you through this lens of distrust, they're primed to feel that you've let them down.

Living by your convictions every day takes discipline, focus, and effort. It can be difficult to be consistent in your behavior and maintain harmony between your personal values and those of the organization. It's not easy to speak up and confront behavior that you know undermines trust in your relationships. It can be gut wrenching to step up and say "I'm sorry" when you've hurt someone. Yet, by staying true to yourself and holding tight to your convictions, you achieve confidence and competence—and expand your personal Capacity for Trust and ability to contribute to Transformative Trust in your organization.

Your life is affected by how you live your convictions, as are the lives of others. When you're clear about your principles, you're able to draw upon them to give new relationships a chance, to give freely to others, and to keep your agreements—or renego-tiate when you honestly can't meet them. Clarity of—and stead-fastness to—your convictions puts you in a position to help others arrive at the same level of clarity within themselves. You create the change you want to see in your organization through model-ing it first yourself. Trust begins with you.

Courage

Courage comes from the French word *coeur*, which means "heart." It takes courage to trust your heart and do what you know is right in the face of adversity. Yet, you need this strength to admit when you've betrayed others or they've betrayed you. You need courage to step into the healing process, take responsibility for your own shortcomings, and work through your pain toward more trustwor-thy relationships. You need courage to create Transformative Trust.

Being courageous allows you contribute more fully to your workplace and the people in it. You let go of the need to control and begin to delegate. You help others learn and grow and inspire them to develop their own inner strength and confidence. You take responsibility for your own mistakes, take the lead in cor-recting them, and encourage others to confront their own fears of failure. You begin to understand that true bravery doesn't lie in fleeting bravado but in substantive action.

It takes courage to trust your heart and do what
you know is right in the face of adversity.

It can be scary to admit you don't know what will happen in the future or to speak up and point out a betrayal resulting from an individual's lapse in integrity or your organization's failure to practice its values. The courage to honor your convictions serves as your guidepost in these tough situations. When you turn away from fear and doubt and toward your inner resilience, you're empowered to tell the truth, honor your intentions, and stick to your values. You have the energy and mental toughness to deliver bad news without spinning it, confront challenges with a spirit of adventure rather than trepidation, and open yourself up to how deeply you care about the opinions of others. Courage breeds trust—both in yourself and in your relationships. Courage breeds Transformative Trust in your organization.

Compassion

Do your co-workers know you care about them? As you attempt to navigate changes in your organization, do you have compassion for those facing uncertainty, confusion, and vulnerability? Are you sensitive to the effects of your words and actions on people who may not be equipped to handle them?

At the transformative level, compassion provides you with an awareness and understanding of others and their struggles. You remember it's not always easy to be human. You consider that at any moment in time, your colleagues are probably doing the absolute best they can do—even if you feel you could have done the job better. You pause and reflect that others often find themselves up against the same walls you've been up against, and they, too, might have produced better work under different circumstances. Compassion encourages you to recognize that, given the opportunity, people want to contribute and make a difference.

Compassion provides you with an awareness and understanding of others and their struggles.

When compassion runs high, your relationships are strengthened, your awareness is enhanced, and your personal Capacity for Trust expands and contributes to the trustworthiness of the entire organization. You recognize and respond to the needs of those who trust you and encourage them to feel safe to talk openly and honestly, to tell the truth, to keep an open heart.

A compassionate approach to your relationships allows you to better appreciate others' intentions, to listen actively, and to be gentle enough with yourself that you put your defenses aside in an effort to take in—and understand—what is being offered. A freer exchange of feedback develops in organizations rich in Transformative Trust as you and others share insights with the higher purposes of growth and learning. As you stretch to become a better version of yourself, you're more able to say "thank you" for these insights—and mean it.

When compassion pervades an organization, you and others understand that although any particular situation, structure, or job description may be temporary, your relationships are constant. You behave accordingly, taking extra steps to avoid breakdowns in trust and immediately working with others toward healing when they occur. This sense of urgency in repairing damaged relationships throws open the door to forgiveness.

The act of forgiveness is an act of creation. You create opportunities to build a more trusting workplace when you and your colleagues release one another from the burdens of blame, guilt, and distrust. You're encouraged to look beyond your pain and no longer hold one another hostage over past betrayals. Your collective energy is freed up for more productive connections, and, although you remember the lessons you learned from letdowns, you don't let them define your current interactions with one another. Forgiveness energizes trust across the organization.

Transformative Trust is fueled by a climate of compassion that allows people to transcend the traditional ways of conducting business. People honor their colleagues' humanity over short-term goals and may even leave formal contracts at the door in favor of more personal understandings. "We've realized that operating strictly by the contract impedes performance," the division manager noted. "We trust one another enough to not rely on them."

Community

When Transformative Trust is present, you understand your individual effort is part of a larger whole or community. You see the underlying meaning and value in what you do, and you take pride in your contribution to the collective effort. You understand that your colleagues are more than people to help you get work done; they're valuable citizens of your workplace community.

At the transformative level, this sense of community promotes openness and honesty in your professional relationships. You feel connected with others through a foundation of trust, and you look forward to cooperating with them. You take responsibility and honor your agreements in the spirit of the relationship, and you feel secure counting on others to get the job done. Through your connection with one another, you shift your focus of operation from *I* to *we*. You believe in yourself and you believe in others. Trust grows; relationships are energized.

Your sense of community shifts your focus from *I* to *we*.

When relationships are taken to the transformative level, you and your co-workers talk to one another. You feel safe discussing deeper issues of interest and matters of importance to you. You and others willingly admit mistakes and mention errors to one another because you know that not doing so would be a betrayal of your community—as well as a lost opportunity for learning and advancement. You feel free to ask for help without fear of looking incompetent or "less than" in the eyes of others. In your connection to your workplace community, you recognize and act on opportunities to give and take, learn and teach, help and be helped.

At the transformative level of trust, you invest in and you create community. You know the best way to achieve individual, team, and organizational objectives is through the collective knowledge, skills, talents, and experiences of your community— people working together in relationship.

Renewal of Trust

Workplace conditions rich in Transformative Trust where you can thrive begin with you. You want to create a work environment where you can use your skills and abilities and tap into your heart and soul fulfilling your potential while also pursuing the organization's business objectives. You create this environment through practicing The Three Cs of trust building behaviors, honoring the Seven Steps for Healing, and leveraging the four catalysts of Transformative Trust. Taken in concert, these actions create an environment in which trust becomes a renewable resource— readily available and continuously replenished.

In organizations with Transformative Trust, trust becomes a renewable resource—readily available and continuously replenished.

You experience this renewal of trust as empowerment to unleash your vast creative and productive energies for the greater good of the organization. You're inspired to bounce back from betrayals, own that you are not a victim, and choose healing over hurt. Together with your colleagues, you find yourself more readily dealing with constant change and challenging situations. The foundation of trust becomes your constant, and you are energized by its presence.

People Want Trust in Their Relationships

You don't know what the future holds for your team or your organization. At best, you can only anticipate the challenges and do your best to prepare for them. You do know, however, that regardless of what the future holds, it will take *people* to address and overcome those challenges. And people, regardless of where they work or what they do, want very much the same thing: to be trusted and to be able to trust in return.

No matter where they work or what they do, people want the same thing: to be trusted and to be able to trust in return.

Are you willing to be a catalyst for transforming the quality of relationships in your organization—and in your life? Are you willing to establish a work environment where everyone is excited about what they do and the people with whom they work? Are you willing to create organizational community where people have an opportunity to express who they are and to be fully present at work? Are you up for the opportunity to take trust to the transformative level?

The raised awareness, language, and understanding you have gained through the Reina Trust & Betrayal Model serves as a framework with which to begin. By trusting in yourself, and choosing to trust in others, you embrace the journey. Trust begins with you.

Trust Building in Action

Reflecting on Your Experience

Think about the four core catalysts of Transformative Trust and the people with whom you work. How would embracing those catalysts transform your relationships, your team, and your organization?

1. What is your conviction to building trusting relationships?

2. How do you exemplify courage?

3. How do you and your co-workers extend compassion to one another on the job?

4. How do you contribute to a sense of community being embodied in your workplace?

Trust Tip ▶ *Trust is built through practicing the behaviors of The Three Cs and working through the Seven Steps for Healing. Trust can be amplified and expanded to Transformative Trust by leveraging its four catalysts: conviction, courage, compassion, and community.*

CHAPTER TEN

Taking Trust to the Next Level

Trust Begins with You

Throughout this book, we've taken you on a journey to discover trust. You've explored what trust means and been introduced to the far-reaching impacts of both its presence and its absence. You've learned about the behaviors that build trust, the level of commitment needed to sustain it, and what to do to repair it when it's been broken. You've been inspired to want trust—and to behave differently in your relationships in order to attract it.

Attracting trust means you are first willing to extend it. Your readiness to extend trust is grounded in your attitude, beliefs, and outlook. Trust begins with you and your ability to align your behavior with sound intentions—an ability that lays a healthy foundation for your relationships. To bring yourself to relationships with others in a trustworthy way, you must first nurture the most central relationship you have—the one you hold with *you*.

In this closing chapter, we turn your attention to the relationship you have with yourself. We support you in expanding your Capacity for Trust and taking trust to the next level by going deeper into this connection through four pathways. They are: Take Care of Yourself, Believe in Yourself, Make Room for

Trust Begins with You

Take Care of Yourself • Believe in Yourself • Make Room for Yourself • Be a Friend to Yourself

Yourself, and Be a Friend to Yourself. It is from this deeper connection with yourself that you take trust to the next level in your relationships, team, organization, and broader community. Trust begins with you.

Take Care of Yourself

The Take Care of Yourself pathway focuses on your relationship with your physical body. Your body is the vehicle that carries you through life. It's the vessel that takes you where you need to go and the conduit through which you connect with others each and every day. You use your body to move, speak, listen, and behave. You rely on it to house and protect your inner spirit, instincts, and core beliefs.

When you compromise the care of your body, you put yourself in a place where it's difficult to hear your inner truth, to tune into your instincts, and to trust yourself to do what needs to be done. When you take care of yourself, you give your body the nourishment, rest, and activity it needs to show up in your relationships in a strong way, to give you what you need to connect, build, and grow over the long term.

The Take Care of Yourself pathway asks you to focus on your primary physical needs for nutrition, rejuvenation, and movement. Our desire isn't to prescribe a specific diet, tell you how many hours of sleep you need, or dictate the most effective workout regime to keep your body fit. We do, however, encourage you to discover the most appropriate self-care formula for yourself. In fact, we propose that doing so is non-negotiable in your quest to develop trustworthy relationships.

Here's why: When you let others down or betray them, you typically don't mean to. The vast majority of the time, you may not even be aware that you've done so. This is because your breach of trust is often the by-product of your disconnection with yourself. You're most vulnerable to living in this disconnected place when you're operating in overdrive: pushing, overextending, overgiving, and otherwise neglecting your own physical well-being. When you're not grounded within a healthy, balanced body, you betray yourself.

We often hear people talk about how little sleep they're getting by on. The compromises to their diet in the name of "this is all I could get my hands on." The neglect of their exercise regimes because they "just don't have the time." It's true that life's circumstances cut into our sleep, nutrition, and workouts. When this neglect becomes a pattern, however, you run the risk of overriding your core, human needs. You put your relationship with yourself in peril, and along with it your relationships with others.

We ask you to consider how you're caring for your physical self. Do you feel energized to build trust in your relationships every day? Or is your body signaling that it's a bit overwhelmed, stretched, and tired? Do you have the energy to jump into your work, life, and relationships with enthusiasm, or are you simply doing what you can to get by?

To walk the Take Care of Yourself pathway, discover what you need to be energized over the course of your day. Contemplate the best sources of nutrition to fuel your body and enliven your senses. Think about the hours of sleep your body actually *requires* to feel alert and vibrant. Pinpoint the type of physical movement that keeps you limber and vital. These personal health practices are the core ingredients to keeping you energized and engaged with life. Everyone's personal health practices will be different: your job is to discover what you need to be healthy and create a rhythm in your schedule that integrates all three components of healthful living.

Rest assured—we are *not* talking about pumping iron, getting washboard abs, or taking in the latest cleansing diet. What we're talking about here are the simple, everyday things your body needs to stay alive, alert, and active. Taking care of yourself at this basic level energizes you. Making the commitment to your personal health practices releases you from pent-up anxieties and nagging illnesses, and grounds you in a centered relationship with yourself. You have more patience, more tolerance, and a greater capacity to learn, grow, and trust.

You owe it to yourself to treat the care of your physical body as a priority. When you do, you're also prioritizing your relationships with others. The more you care for yourself, the more you have to give. The more you deepen your relationship with your physical being, the better positioned you are to take your relationships with others to the next level.

Believe in Yourself

The Believe in Yourself pathway focuses on your relationship with your inner spirit. You are a unique human being, and there is no one else like you in the world. You have unique gifts, talents, and perspectives that you bring to your relationships with others. You have experience and knowledge that position you to make the world a better place. The health of your inner spirit relies on your respect for this innate uniqueness and the positive intention with which you bring yourself to your life.

Consider all of the roles you play in the work you do and the life you lead. You are a number of things to a number of people: co-worker, boss, employee, customer, sister, brother, son, wife, father, partner, neighbor. Contemplate your contribution to these relationships—to the teams you work with, the community you serve, and the family you nurture. Think about the difference your efforts have made to your networks over the course of a lifetime.

Next, imagine the positive things you'd hear your closest connections say about you if only you'd listen. Would they say you are kind, brave, smart, or generous? Would they sing praises of your ethical toughness, devotion to quality, or admirable dependability? Would you be able to accept these positive things your friends, colleagues, and family members say about you? Would you be able to accept that you are appreciated just for being who you are?

As you walk the Believe in Yourself pathway, we ask you to consider accepting the words of appreciation from others as the clearest reflection of your inner spirit. Be willing to accept that those who know you best are in the best position to see the contributions you make. That they're qualified to hold up the mirror and show you your true value. We encourage you to accept their expressions of gratitude, to claim others' positive perceptions of your strengths as inner truths you can hold close as personal affirmations. No one can take these inner truths away from you—ever. Especially when you need them most, during the tough times.

Because there *will* be tough times. There will be hurts and letdowns. Others will betray you and you will betray them. Unintentional breaches of trust will occur. When they do, you may find yourself second-guessing your capabilities and doubting your contributions to others—and perhaps even to life itself. In the complexity of relationships, it's easy to lose sight of the most cherished parts of yourself—your inner truths. Yet, it's during these times you most need to believe in yourself, remember who you are, and be proud of the value you bring to the world.

Life is dynamic. There are times when it seems like it's in your favor and times when it doesn't. Your belief in yourself helps you move through difficult situations, tests of character, and energy leaks sprung by the natural rhythms of trust and betrayal. In these times of tribulation, we urge you to tune into what you know to be true about yourself; to leverage these reference points as anchors within your shadow of doubt and have faith that they will enable you to move through your pain and disappointment and learn to trust again.

Your belief in yourself can form a steady cadence that drives your movement through this world. It can help you honor yourself: your inner courage, your willingness to take risks and open doors, your ability to be vulnerable and extend forgiveness. It can put up a strong barrier between you and those who would ask you to compromise your inner spirit and what you know to be right.

Your belief in yourself can illuminate your way forward when you're surrounded by uncertainty or confusion. When you believe that you are a naturally caring person, that you want to do the right thing, and that you are on a search to become the best version of yourself, you infuse your inner spirit with what is most essential—strength and resilience as you move through the demanding business of trust building.

In the Believe in Yourself pathway, we ask you to think carefully about the language you use to communicate with yourself. Do your words reflect a positive inner belief in yourself? If not, reach for the words that create this positive belief. Ground yourself in a healthy outlook about what you bring to this world. Take pride in your unique contributions. Everyone needs to be seen and understood for who they are. You can answer this need for yourself.

Make Room for Yourself

The Make Room for Yourself pathway focuses on your need for time to tune into yourself. When you make room for yourself, you create the space you need to integrate what you've discovered about your approach to relationships into your greater awareness. You become more conscious of what you need for support and guide yourself to override your knee-jerk reactions and "business as usual" attitudes to both life and work. You rely on this pathway to shift your perceptions, develop wisdom, and honor your highest intentions.

On the quiet Make Room for Yourself pathway, we ask you to create space within which you connect to yourself. We urge you to pause, breathe, and reflect. When you hear "make room for yourself," you may be inclined to think in big terms: full days off, a weekend unplugged from email, extended vacations, even several-month sabbaticals. Although it's important to make these big "rooms" for yourself, it's even more vital to create a series of little "rooms" throughout the course of each day where you take a moment to catch your breath and reflect. Creating these little rooms for yourself—even just a few minutes each—can give you the gifts of peace, focus, and perspective.

These gifts appear because when you build space to just "be," you pause the grind, the expectations, and the constant demand to give to others. Instead, you give to yourself. You remember who you are. You sink back into your own skin. You allow yourself to tune in to your thoughts and feelings. We encourage you to absorb the clarity that comes during these moments of stillness. Welcome the perspective and wisdom you gain; they represent your truth.

Walking the Make Room for Yourself pathway means you must be intentional in setting time for *you*. This requires you to be mindful of your tendency to over commitment. To say no or not right now, when saying yes would put you into hyper-drive. To stop racing toward the future or lamenting about the past, and step away from the buzz of the electronic world, even if just for a few moments.

Building this commitment to make room for yourself doesn't have to be arduous. Even two minutes can be enough time to reclaim your sense of self. Arriving early for a meeting can give you the room you need to center, remember why you're doing what you're doing, and to set your intentions for how you want to show up as you connect with others. Spending a little extra time after a conference call to refill your tea and process your day can be enough. It's not the grandeur of the "room" that's important—it's the benefit of the silence and stillness you find there, the presence you gain.

The first step along the Make Room for Yourself pathway is to give yourself permission to take the time you need for yourself. Remember, this time isn't selfish or decadent. It is *responsible*. Trust begins with you. When you connect with yourself, you're more able to forge trustworthy connections with others.

Be a Friend to Yourself

The Be a Friend to Yourself pathway focuses on being kind to yourself—on cutting yourself some slack, remembering you are a work in progress, and giving yourself credit for doing your best at any moment in time. Your ability to be a friend to yourself influences your ability to build trustworthy friendships with others.

Are you your own worst enemy? We're all usually harder on ourselves than anybody else. When others beat themselves up, how do you respond? We'd imagine you say things like "Don't be so hard on yourself. Look at what you've accomplished. You'll only improve next time." We encourage you to reimagine your relationship with yourself and infuse it with the kindness, understanding, and the steady encouragement you give to those whom you most respect, trust, or love.

In your friendships with others, you support their growth and progress—even when that progress is gained from the deeper wisdom generated by letdowns and disappointments. You support their ambition—even when they wind up biting off "more than they can chew." In the space of friendship, you encourage others to reach for opportunities to achieve, yet provide a "soft landing" of compassionate reassurance if they fall short. You don't let your friends speak negatively of themselves when they stretch yet miss the mark. You don't let them beat themselves up when life asks for more than they're able to give. You don't make them wrong as people. In fact, you remind them of who they are and celebrate their efforts.

As you walk the Be a Friend to Yourself pathway, we ask you to show up for yourself the way you show up for others. Support your own opportunities to learn, grow, and achieve. Yes, it's important to tell the truth and take ownership when you don't get

the results you're looking for. But it's equally important to recognize that shortcomings aren't flaws in your character; they're
little proofs of your humanity. Friends don't stop supporting one
another when their imperfections come to light. Neither should
you stop supporting yourself when you struggle.

So, how do you travel the Be a Friend to Yourself pathway?
What does being a friend to *you* look like? How do you show
up for yourself as your own best friend? First, cut yourself some
slack. Stop breathing down your own neck. Get off your own
back. When your inner voice spouts off that you're not good
enough, tell it that it's wrong. Back away from your tendencies
toward perfection and recognize that you are a work in progress—just like everyone else in this world. That you're growing in
awareness and consciousness. That at any given time, you're doing
the best you can with what you have and from where you stand.
But above all, be kind to yourself. Take a step forward with the
knowledge that next time you will do better.

Consider how you extend kindness to others across the
breadth of your relationships and mimic those efforts toward
yourself. Gift yourself with gentle reminders, little encourage-
ments, big acknowledgements, and positive affirmations.

Give yourself permission to take care of your body through
better nutrition, deeper rest, and more satisfying physical activity. Create daily reminders of what you know to be true about the
value you bring to this world. Build pauses into your day in which
you set your intentions and reclaim your perspective. Give yourself these kindnesses just as sincerely and frequently as you would
give them to a friend and watch your relationship with *you*—with
all of you—thrive and influence the health and trustworthiness of
your relationships with others.

Final Thoughts

As we close this final chapter of *Trust and Betrayal in the Workplace*, we'd like to give you a piece of inspiration to take with you: The energy you need to build, sustain, and rebuild trust in your life is always available to you. As you walk the four pathways that deepen your relationship with yourself—Take Care of Yourself, Believe in Yourself, Make Room for Yourself, and Be a Friend to Yourself—you honor you and the intentions you bring to your relationships.

Walking the pathways support you in tapping your inner truth when you take care of your body, mind, and spirit. You discover your ability to put your self-critic on mute, turn up the volume on your intuition, and move through the world in a fluid manner. You develop the talent to view yourself holistically, positively, and compassionately. You visualize a new reality for yourself founded on the serene confidence that you can transform your relationships.

Trust is a vital force in your connections with others and with yourself. Walking the pathways given to you in this chapter creates alignment with this force and grants you access to the infinite energy available to you in your efforts to forge trustworthy relationships. With this alignment, you stay true to yourself through the challenges and disappointments life brings. You bring yourself to others with an open mind and compassionate heart, and, in the end, wind up receiving more than you give. Trust begins with you.

The energy you need to build, sustain, and
rebuild trust is always available to you.

Index

Acknowledgments

We have been surrounded by a circle of people who have trusted and believed in us, trusted in the contribution this book will make to others, and who have provided invaluable support in bringing this work to fruition.

From Berrett-Koehler, we thank Steve Piersanti for embracing our vision of this third edition, for his thoughtful guidance on shaping its editorial direction, and for challenging us to sharpen our voice. We thank Kristen Frantz, a longtime adviser who provides steady direction and friendship. We thank Tricia Molly and Pat Buehler, whose feedback grounded our approach to this project. We thank the Berrett-Koehler staff for their trust in what this book would bring.

Jill Swenson helped us to refine the structure of this edition to bring clarity. Allyson Baughman helped us to take it to the next level and infuse it with our hearts and souls.

Jennifer Beverage brought creative insights and fresh perspective on how to visually reshape the trust concepts embedded throughout this book. Bob von Elgg brought them to life by infusing them with his artistic imaging.

Mark Levy guided us to share our personal experiences with trust and betrayal in order to empower others to do so.

Pauline Hodgdon anchors the diverse elements of our day-to-day business with loyalty and steadfastness. Amanda Fallon provides faithful support in navigating the complexity of research and analysis in service to our clients and us.

We have been privileged to work with thousands of people in hundreds of organizations. From them we have learned the power of trust and the hope for future relationships in organizations. We bring ourselves in service to them and we are served in return. We thank them for embracing our work and using it to build trust in their relationships with themselves and others.

Finally, we give thanks to the process of life for bringing us together and for providing us with the opportunity to make a contribution to the development of trust in relationships in all walks of life. People often ask us "How do you two do it? As a husband and wife, how do you both work and live together?" The truth? We would not have it any other way. Together, we continue.

About the Authors

 Dennis Reina, PhD and Michelle Reina, PhD are cofounders of Reina, A Trust Building Consultancy: Transforming Workplaces Through Trust. In the field of organizational trust, Dennis and Michelle are considered pioneers.

When they started consulting together in 1991, Dennis and Michelle's practice focused on how to create self-directed work teams and repair broken change efforts. At the time, a few people *talked* about how critical trust was in accomplishing those things, but no one gave *explicit instructions* on how to build trust or recover trust when it had been broken. Dennis and Michelle went to work on closing that gap. They began a comprehensive, "in the trenches" study of trust building. They then applied their learning to building high-performing, trust-fueled cultures in organizations around the world.

Through more than two decades of research, consulting, and frontline experience, the Reinas have developed a Trust Building system that includes statistically valid trust measurements at the organization, team, leader, and individual levels. They also develop thoroughly customized solutions to support people in their efforts to build more trustworthy relationships.

Sought after consultants, workshop leaders, speakers, and executive coaches, Michelle and Dennis have worked with thousands of people in more than two hundred organizations around the globe.

Trust building is not just what Dennis and Michelle *do* professionally. It's their life's work. They bring trust, healing, and renewal to the world from the inside out. They find particular satisfaction in how their clients integrate their Trust Building concepts into all aspects of life. Time and again, people tell them: "Not only has my company's culture transformed, my relationships outside of work have been transformed, too. I've been able to teach these trust building principles to my family and friends. My life has been changed."

Dennis and Michelle's clients include American Express, Ben & Jerry's, Dartmouth-Hitchcock Medical Center, Harvard University, Johnson & Johnson, Lincoln Financial Group, MillerCoors, Nokia, Toyota, Turner Broadcasting, Walt Disney World, the US Army, and the US Treasury Department.

The Reinas have written two award-winning, best-selling business books, which have been published in multiple languages: *Trust and Betrayal in the Workplace: Building Effective Relationships in Your Organization* and *Rebuilding Trust in the Workplace: Seven Steps to Renew Confidence, Commitment, and Energy.*

The Reinas' Trust Building work has been written about in Bloomberg *BusinessWeek*, *Harvard Management Update*, the *New York Times*, the *Wall Street Journal*, *Time* magazine, and *USA Today*, and it has been featured on TV and radio networks such as CNBC and CNN.

Dennis and Michelle have received several thought leadership awards, including the World HRD Congress Global Strategic Leadership Award and Top 100 Thought Leaders in Trustworthy Business.

Working with Reina, A Trust Building Consultancy

Dennis and Michelle Reina, cofounders of Reina, A Trust Building Consultancy, know that trust is essential for high workplace performance. Trust, in fact, is a key part of organizational innovation, teamwork, collaboration, and accountability. Unfortunately, when trust is broken, people often do the opposite of what's needed. They withdraw commitment, become judgmental, and withhold information.

Since 1991, Dennis and Michelle Reina have helped people at all levels of responsibility turn loss into opportunity, build trust, surpass business goals, and transform culture . . . making organizations places where everyone can come together in openness and possibility in order to do their best work.

Dennis and Michelle bring their Trust Building work to organizations in four ways: through consulting, keynote speaking, coaching, and training workshops.

Consulting: Through Reina, A Trust Building Consultancy, Dennis and Michelle provide practical, measurable, and fully customized Trust Building strategies to drive initiatives such as employee engagement and satisfaction, change and transition, mergers and acquisitions, team and leadership development, innovation, creativity, risk taking, collaboration and bottom line improvement.

Keynote speaking: Dennis and Michelle captivate audiences with their heartfelt, informative, and engaging keynote speeches—presentations that help people at all levels of responsibility learn proven strategies to build and rebuild trust in their relationships to achieve their goals. Together and independently, Dennis and Michelle are available for keynote speeches, conferences, and seminars anywhere in the world.

Executive coaching: Through a process of inquiry, reflection, and assessment Dennis and Michelle help senior leaders identify and understand how their trustworthiness impacts their effectiveness and business results. Using their Trust Building approach, they work with clients to pinpoint their business needs and identify behavioral obstacles that are preventing leaders from being more successful and going to the next level.

Training workshops: Reina, A Trust Building Consultancy provides hands-on Trust WorkOut sessions that transfer capability to participants, enabling them to put Trust Building principles and tools into action to resolve real issues in real time.

Whether you're in an organization experiencing trust-related issues, or you're in a highly functioning organization that realizes strong trust is a way of intensifying your competitive advantage, Dennis and Michelle Reina can help.

The Differences You'll Experience Working with Reina, A Trust Building Consultancy

- Trust work shouldn't be a mere teaching tool or abstract feel-good exercise. At Reina, trust work is done in service of your organization's measurable business goals and cultural transformation.

- Trust work shouldn't be based on blind assumption and opinion. At Reina, trust issues are pinpointed through a comprehensive, statistically valid and reliable assessment protocol.

- Defining what trust looks like should be only a first step toward renewal. At Reina, sound methodology helps you rebuild trust from mistrust and betrayal.

- An organization shouldn't be beholden to a consulting firm to keep positive change going. At Reina, methods are customized to suit your goals and transfer capability by teaching you how to use the methods on your own. This learning empowers you to *sustain* the strong trust levels you develop in your work with Reina.

- Trust work is critical work, so you don't want to deal with a firm for whom trust is a sideline or marketing stance. Dennis and Michelle Reina have been rebuilding trust in organizations for twenty-five years. It's the only work they do. It's their life's work.

To learn more, please schedule an appointment to speak with Dennis or Michelle Reina at www.reinatrustbuilding.com; reina@reinatrustbuilding.com; or 802-253-8808.

Also by Dennis and Michelle Reina

Rebuilding Trust in the Workplace

Seven Steps to Renew Confidence, Commitment, and Energy

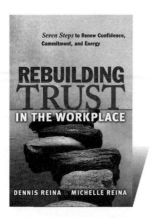

Winner of the Axiom Silver Business Book Award in Business Ethics and the Nautilus Silver Book Award in Business Relationships

As important as trust is, it is frequently broken in the workplace, sometimes intentionally, but most often unintentionally. No matter the cause, when trust is broken, people often do the opposite of what's needed: they withdraw commitment, become judgmental, and withhold information. And they seldom know how to begin restoring it.

Instead of pulling back, people need to step into the challenge while acknowledging and working through the issues. This is the only book that provides a tested, research-based approach for rebuilding trust at work and the first to give equal weight to what to do when you are the one who violated someone else's trust.

Trust will be built, and trust will be broken. Broken trust is simply the ordinary outcome of people interacting with one another. What's extraordinary is the commitment to rebuilding trust. This book offers a proven, compassionate seven-step process to heal broken trust, renew relationships, and transform your workplace.

Paperback, 192 pages, ISBN 978-1-60509-372-7
PDF ebook, ISBN 978-1-60509-374-1

Berrett–Koehler Publishers, Inc.
www.bkconnection.com   **800.929.2929**

Berrett–Koehler
Publishers

Berrett-Koehler is an independent publisher dedicated to an ambitious mission: *connecting people and ideas to create a world that works for all.*

We believe that to truly create a better world, action is needed at all levels—individual, organizational, and societal. At the individual level, our publications help people align their lives with their values and with their aspirations for a better world. At the organizational level, our publications promote progressive leadership and management practices, socially responsible approaches to business, and humane and effective organizations. At the societal level, our publications advance social and economic justice, shared prosperity, sustainability, and new solutions to national and global issues.

A major theme of our publications is "Opening Up New Space." Berrett-Koehler titles challenge conventional thinking, introduce new ideas, and foster positive change. Their common quest is changing the underlying beliefs, mindsets, institutions, and structures that keep generating the same cycles of problems, no matter who our leaders are or what improvement programs we adopt.

We strive to practice what we preach—to operate our publishing company in line with the ideas in our books. At the core of our approach is stewardship, which we define as a deep sense of responsibility to administer the company for the benefit of all of our "stakeholder" groups: authors, customers, employees, investors, service providers, and the communities and environment around us.

We are grateful to the thousands of readers, authors, and other friends of the company who consider themselves to be part of the "BK Community." We hope that you, too, will join us in our mission.

A BK Business Book

This book is part of our BK Business series. BK Business titles pioneer new and progressive leadership and management practices in all types of public, private, and nonprofit organizations. They promote socially responsible approaches to business, innovative organizational change methods, and more humane and effective organizations.

Berrett–Koehler
Publishers

Connecting people and ideas
to create a world that works for all

Dear Reader,

Thank you for picking up this book and joining our worldwide community of Berrett-Koehler readers. We share ideas that bring positive change into people's lives, organizations, and society.

To welcome you, we'd like to offer you a free e-book. You can pick from among twelve of our bestselling books by entering the promotional code **BKP92E** here: http://www.bkconnection.com/welcome.

When you claim your free e-book, we'll also send you a copy of our e-news-letter, the *BK Communiqué*. Although you're free to unsubscribe, there are many benefits to sticking around. In every issue of our newsletter you'll find

- A free e-book
- Tips from famous authors
- Discounts on spotlight titles
- Hilarious insider publishing news
- A chance to win a prize for answering a riddle

Best of all, our readers tell us, "Your newsletter is the only one I actually read." So claim your gift today, and please stay in touch!

Sincerely,

Charlotte Ashlock
Steward of the BK Website

Questions? Comments? Contact me at bkcommunity@bkpub.com.